◦❧ Book One ❧◦

## Letters From the Inner Self

# The Indwelling Spirit

*Timely Messages for the Souls of Earth*

# Praise for The Indwelling Spirit

This book is filled with love, clarity, and reverence. A breath of Light and air. It is a wonderful offering! Truly Inspiring! What a gift! It is food for the soul. --*Allan Cohen, Author of 20 books including* The Dragon Doesn't Live Here Anymore

This inspiring, timely book opens the door to a Soul Awakening that if embraced, can create a joyful life filled with Love, Harmony and Beauty. --*John Gray, Author of* Men Are From Mars, Women Are From Venus

Spend some time each day with these beautiful writings and feel your life rise on wings of love. --*Gay Hendricks, Author of* Conscious Living, *Co-author with Kathlyn Hendricks of* Conscious Loving

This is information that nourishes the soul. --*Wayne Dyer, Author of over thirty books including* The Power of Intention.

This is more than a book. It is a blessing. Divinely inspired, flowing with poetic wisdom directly into the human soul, it opens you to your deepest truth with love and compassion. —*Leonard Laskow, M.D., Author of* Healing With Love

Aurora Juliana Ariel graces us with the wisdom and inspiration of her clear channel to Spirit. The truths we hear in her writing are echoes of the free, expansive and radiant being that is the Eternal Self. We are fortunate to have pure souls like Aurora on this planet to remind us of who we really are. Her book is a great gift for those who would travel the path of spiritual transcendence, awakening and its abiding peace. --*Kamala Allen, Ph.D., Author of* A Woman's Guide to Opening A Man's Heart

Words cannot adequately express the wisdom, majesty and beauty of the inspired information in this book. As I read the uplifting and empowering words, I "feel" how important it is that this wondrous message be distributed far and wide to awaken and empower the millions of people that have been waiting for these words all their lives. It is sacred work! Humanity is at a time of ripeness for this awakening. This book of spiritual teaching and encouragement can help facilitate this awakening. This exquisitely beautiful work will truly enlighten the world. --*Sharon Huffman, Contributing Author of Ten Traits of Highly Effective Teachers, Chicken Soup For the Soul, Gratitude: A Way of Life, and Attitudes of Gratitude*

An oracle of inspirational guidance for the soul, this book is uniquely crafted as a recipe for Awakening Souls, inspiring them to live a Divine Existence as their Authentic Selves.--*Mirra Rose, Spiritual Teacher, Healer*

AURORA JULIANA ARIEL PhD

❖ Book One ❖

Letters From the Inner Self

# THE INDWELLING SPIRIT

*TIMELY MESSAGES FOR THE SOULS OF EARTH*

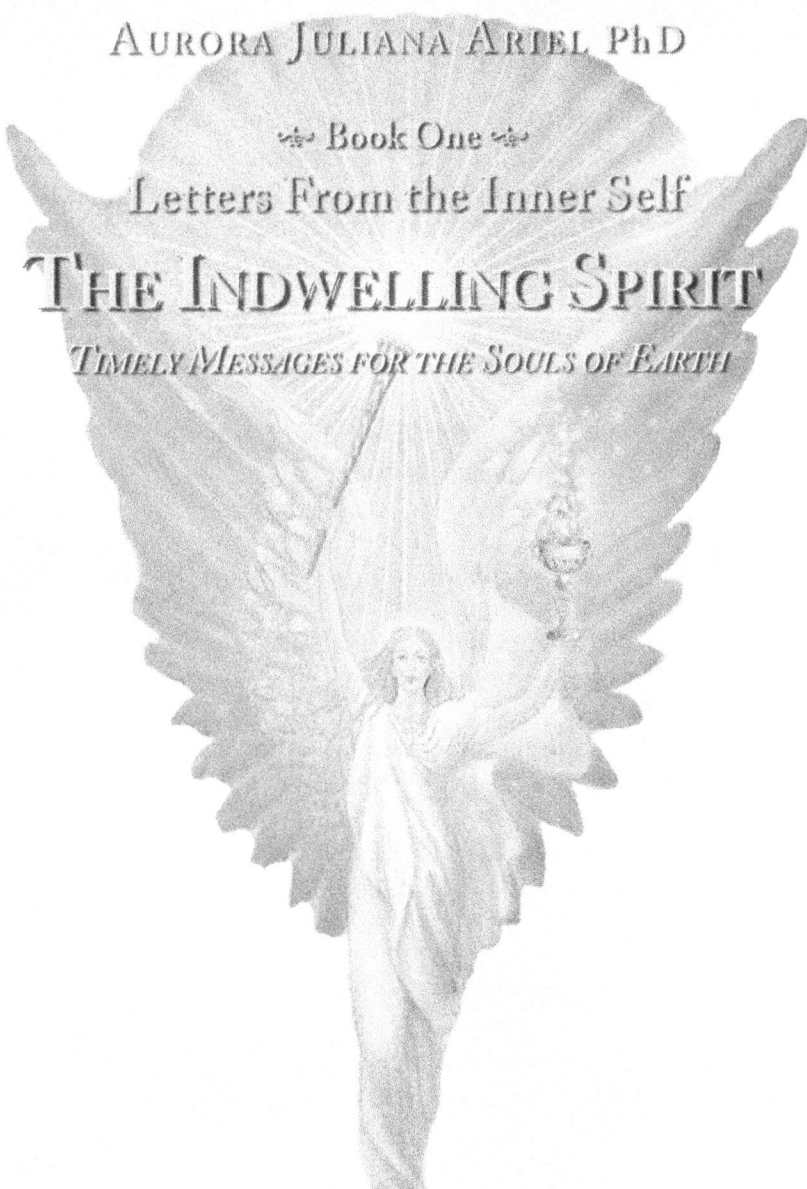

An Illumined Pathway to
Freedom, Enlightenment and Peace

## A New Frontier In Multimedia Arts
*Inspired Music, Books, & Films*

Publisher: AEOS, Inc.
PO Box 433, Malibu, California 90265
Ph: 310-591-8799   Fax: 413-521-8799
Email: Info@AEOS.ws
Website: http://www.AEOS.ws

Interior Design by Kareen Ross
Cover Art by Marius Michael George
Bio Photos by Monique Feil and Christian Cooper
Art Direction, Cover Design by Aurora Juliana Ariel

Letters From the Inner Self: The Indwelling Spirit
Copyright ©2011 by Aurora Juliana Ariel, PhD.

Printed in the USA
by Lightening Source and Create Space

FIRST EDITION
*Library of Congress*
ISBN 978-0-9847571-0-7

# Dedication

I dedicate this book to

Awakening Souls Worldwide.

May you be blessed, nurtured and enriched by

these Letters from the Inner Self,

Inspired to fulfill your highest destiny potential and

Live in Heaven on Earth in your own life experience,

helping restore Eden on Earth.

# Acknowledgments

## With the deepest gratitude
## I acknowledge and thank...

The many incredible teachers who have shed light on my pathway too numerous to name.

My Inner Divine Self, Divine Master Teachers, and Heavenly Sponsors.

My beautiful children, Mariah, Araphiel, Gabriel, and Aradeus, for your love, support, and unwavering belief in me.

Marc Ivey, Tara Grace, and Joe Sugarman for your support of AEOS and the birth of my life's work.

Violet Flames: Susan Saltz, Elizabeth Lutz, and Bernadette Vazquez of my Sacred Healing Circle, for your loving presence and support of my Highest Destiny Fulfillment.

My Soul Family... who have walked the Sacred Journey with me, delving deeply and rising to ever new heights... Arya Bruce BecVar, Melea Moir, Bernadette and Chester Jagiello. I am grateful for your continual love and support.

My Ojai Family... Thank you for all your love and friendship during my retreat time in the 'Sacred Valley' while completing the edit of this book: Cathy Norman, Steve, Steven Krauthoff, Peter Sterling, Crystal, Bernadette and Chester.

Beautiful Aspen, my favorite place to write midst awe inspiring beauty, always a source of inspiration on my journey. Thank you for opening your homes to me, Clay Colver and Joanie Klar Bruce as I did the last edit on this book.

My Maui Author Group: Shakti Navran, Linda Deslauriers, Toby Neal, and Rona Miller for your continued insights, inspiration and support.

# Contents

## Part Three: Addendum

The resounding echo
through this book is that we are loved.
Through this LOVE of the Indwelling Spirit
we are inspired to see, know, and love ourselves
in the way that God loves us.
When we love ourselves absolutely,
we give ourselves our best life.
Embracing ourselves from this Divine Perspective,
we live Sacred and Abundant Lives
accessing the Great Power Within.
As we consecrate the moments of our existence to a Higher Purpose,
we allow the Divine Plan for our life to fulfill itself in and through us.
Living in the Miracle Consciousness, we enter the Miraculous Life,
A sacred and richly fulfilling existence where we
uncover Life's Sacred Mysteries
witnessing to the majesty and glory of our
Authentic Self as we walk our Highest Destiny Path.
A Guide to Freedom, Enlightenment and Peace,
the writings in this book inspire us
upon an Illumined Pathway to realize our Full Potential.
They unveil the Secret Code to our True Destiny.
These Sacred Writings reveal the Majesty and Power of
Our Innate Divinity and speak to the extraordinary mission
we have come to Earth to fulfill at this significant time.
Eloquently written through Letters from the Inner Self,
this book is destined to help awaken and inspire humanity
in its next evolutionary leap in consciousness,
Igniting Positive World Change and a
planetary transformation unparalleled in history
that can restore Eden on Earth.

# Introduction

In my early teens I became aware of a part of me I have come to know as the Inner Self. Learning early on to follow its guidance unfailingly, I was able to access this place of deep Inner Wisdom to assist me in every challenging situation. This led me into ever new arenas of self-discovery and self-awareness.

It is from this place of Inner Wisdom that I have learned to write, accessing a never-ending wealth of inspiration and knowledge. In bringing forth this body of work, I have relied solely on this Inner Awareness, continually moving my conscious mind out of the way so my Inner Self could bring forth her inspired message in its purest form. To what degree I have been able to accomplish this, must then, be assessed by the reader.

There have been times when an unquenchable fire to write would well up inside of me until I could do nothing else. Waiting for these times became an art and then allowing its full creative expression became the way this book has been brought forth.

Each quote preceding the chapters has come from this same inspiration. It was as if, through my alliance with the Inner Self, the portals of Heaven were opened to higher realms where Jewels of Wisdom flowed forth with incredible insights on the portent of this body of knowledge and its application for a world in transition. In this set of Letters, this inspiration came from the Indian Sage, Babaji, whose presence was a very real and tangible experience the moment I sat down to write. His quotes are powerful and poignant, adding significantly to this body of work.

While these pages embody what I have come to know as "truth," they remain largely the inspired work of this Sacred Part of me. Therefore I lay no claims what I have brought forth is everyone's truth. I simply offer it as a gift of my Inner Self with the hope that many people throughout the world will drink from this well and find healing, nourishment, and peace. My prayer is, it fulfills its mission, providing you with an experiential journey that awakens you more fully to your Authentic Self, so you can help restore the Edenic Way of Life by anchoring Heaven on Earth in your own life experience.

It is essential for you, the reader, to find your own truth, embark upon your own inner journey of self-discovery and connect with your own Inner Self. The only real meaning any of us can gain from our life's path is what is revealed to us in this most sacred and personal way, for what we can experience we can know. How much richer this personal experience is than merely accepting the beliefs conveyed or passed down by others.

I believe True Freedom comes when we individually access the TRUTH within us from this deep place of Inner Knowing. Aligning with our Inner Self, we awaken to our best teacher and find our greatest truths. Our life becomes a miraculous journey, witnessing to the ever-present beauty, majesty, and grace, which is our true Soul Essence.

From this place of illumination, we can minister to the parts of self who have been imprinted with a shadow awareness. Healing and transforming these 'Inner Aspects,' we can experience a profound healing at the deepest levels of our psyches, which changes our thoughts, feelings and behaviors and then transforms the world around us. Over many years I developed a way to do this which I call TheQuest.

This book is a guide to Self-discovery. It is a Life Mastery Course allowing you to handle the most challenging situations with a grace and understanding that is rare. It is a Way of Life. It is a training, if applied, can totally transform your life as it did mine. It is a Sacred Journey, leading you into the deepest parts of yourself where you find your Inner Self smiling radiantly as he/she welcomes you home.

When you find the Inner Self, you begin to relax completely knowing you are safe. You learn to trust its Inner Guidance and follow it unfailingly. You find your Inner Self has all the wisdom and insights your conscious mind lacks. It holds the key to your Highest Destiny Fulfillment. It is then you realize the greatest gift you could ever give yourself is to relinquish your temporal power and limited awareness to the Inner Self so it can manifest the glory of its vision in and through you. When you do that, you are on your Highest Destiny Path and your life begins to change miraculously.

Divine Synchronicities grace your existence and life becomes a magical adventure. You relax deeply into yourself, knowing you are loved. You realize you are in the embrace of a Benevolent Universe that wills only good for you. You are able to discern the deeper meaning of your life experiences and how everything you pass through, no matter how challenging, is designed for your greatest soul growth, refinement, and advancement. That is when you enter a deep Inner Peace and live the Sacred Life destined for you.

# Part One

Letters from the Inner Self

# The Journey Begins

In 1998 at the beautiful villa, Shanti Aloha, where I lived on Maui, I was inspired to read the book, *The Artists Way*, and to put into practice the morning pages, which were to be written each day. This was an exercise to unblock the creative flow and enhance creative expression. The idea was to allow whatever wanted to be written to flow forth uncensored. This was a time each day to pour out feelings, to share deeply, whether a joyful or painful expression. It was Sacred Time.

When I sat down on my computer excited to begin my first morning pages, an incredible thing happened. The words poured forth, *"At last a voice in your busy world."* I was stunned! An insightful voice continued, drawing me into a magical inner world. I was being spoken to directly from my Inner Self who invited me on an extraordinary journey.

She said, *"If you should take this trek with me, opening up to my magic and gifts, your life will change completely. It will look so different than anything you have witnessed before, because it will no longer be structured upon that which is illusion from an illusionary world of beliefs. Lost in a world of illusion you have often sought me not knowing truly where to find me and now you know."* And so, the incredible journey began and I was never the same.

In this first message she shared, *"I am the one you have longed for in your Quest for Eternal Youth. I am the one you have striven to become in your Quest for Enlightenment. At last you are here in My Abode and I bid you welcome. Welcome and come in."*

The Inner Self helped me realize, while my striving for spiritual attainment had largely been an outer quest, the Ultimate Quest was an inner journey to the center of my Self, a journey into the heart of who I truly am. She showed me when I am my Authentic Self, I am enlightened. I am fully conscious and aware.

She went on to say, *"Feast upon the many Delights I am here to share with you. Enter Joy for the first time in many years of fortitude and striv-*

*ing. Be at Peace in my Garden of Delight, drinking in the Sweet Fragrance and Nectar of Everlasting Bliss, the Divine Elixir, which is Life Eternal and all the precious qualities that are jewels in their own right. Access these treasures on a mystical treasure hunt with me, for I grant you permission to enter the Garden with me and I am here to guide you every step of the way. I am your Inner Creative Self."*

Inner Creative Self! Those words resounded through me. She had revealed herself as the inner creative part of me and invited me into the Garden. Could that be a metaphor for the lost Garden of Eden souls had departed from in our distant past? I was intrigued.

I had never imagined, as I sat down to write my first Morning Pages, I would be embarking on an incredible adventure, nor did I fathom the depths that journey would take me. I had been determined to unlock my creative expression and that intention had unlocked my Inner Creative Self. I had tapped into the Inner Self many times, but obviously, in my full and busy life, I had failed to truly comprehend the majesty and grace of this illumined part of me. Now she was ready to take me on a journey, to personally educate and awaken me, and I was determined to make room for her to be more fully present in my life.

For the next two years I received the most precious letters from the Inner Self. Each day I printed them out on my favorite rainbow paper and lay them reverently on my bedside table. Each night before I went to sleep, I would read them again. I found them powerful, enlightening and life transforming.

Day after day, her wisdom was impeccable, her guidance clear, her understanding astute. She led me deep into myself, helping me uncover the stranglehold of human patterning that had made it impossible to follow her guidance. She helped me see how the driving parts of me, though noble intentioned, were still the human voice having its way. I found the Super Achiever and Workaholic parts of me, with their humanitarian principles and spiritual philosophies, were nothing more than programs running from my subconscious, filling my daily existence to overflowing to where I barely had a life. I balanced this new inner awareness with inner work, applying TheQuest as patterns arose. In each self-counseling, I was clearing the way for my Inner Creative Self to have her perfect expression in and through me.

I learned the Inner Creative Self was a still, quieter voice. To hear her, I had to be silent. I had to rearrange my life so I could be available, open, ready and listening. I had to fill my life with quiet moments, to give myself a lot of space just to be. This was an incredible training and area of Self Mastery I had not sought.

I found it was not easy to follow the guidance of the Inner Self. It took a lot of shifting internally to be really present for her. This amazed me. I thought I had always been attuned to my Inner Awareness, but the truth was, I was a very driven person. Driven in ways that looked great to the outer world, but in truth, they were wearing me out and I had little time for myself.

By the time the letters completed, I was a very changed person. Two years had passed and I had recreated my life to be more spacious and thus, more peaceful. I had learned to listen for those moments of inspiration and ride that creative wave expressing my deepest self. I could still accomplish and make things happen. I was still grounded, centered, and responsible and I was so much freer than I had ever been with so much more joy. I had learned to treasure the many gifts of this powerful part of me. I had learned about True Power, a quiet power that does not need to make a big show or have a big push in the world. I learned how to manifest easily and effortlessly.

As I journeyed deeper into this miraculous life, I began to see the magic of what she had been speaking of. I had stepped out of the driver's seat and had allowed her to take over and she completely blew my mind. I was having the most incredible experiences. Miracles became commonplace. Each day was filled with synchronicities, incredible meetings, amazing alliances. I no longer had to work hard or strive to accomplish my goals. I simply was manifesting a Higher Vision for my life, living in the Miracle Consciousness, guided unerringly by the Indwelling Spirit.

Each letter has been a precious jewel and altogether a garland of wisdom and love shedding light on my pathway. They are gifts beyond earthly treasures. Over the two years they were released, they gave me alchemical keys essential to my landmark research and pioneering work, which I am now offering to the world in myriad forms, a sacred and holy purpose that is a great joy to fulfill. The Inner Creative Self showed me finally these letters were destined to be released as books.

In book one and two, the Inner Self speaks eloquently on the Art of Sacred Living, giving keys to living in the Miracle Consciousness that initiates you into the Miraculous Life. In books three and four, she shares timely insights on how to live an Abundant Life, anchoring Heaven on Earth in your own life experience. This, for many in the spiritual community is a lost art after millennia of religious doctrine that inspired self-denial, poverty, and lack as a way to spiritual enlightenment, both in the East and West.

I have seen visions of what these inspired messages will mean to the spiritual communities of the world. It is a healing salve for those who are moving out of the old paradigm, with its limited awareness and life expression, to the New Archetype of 'Wealth Wedded With Spirituality,' which is being birthed at this significant time through Awakening Souls worldwide.

The Inner Creative Self taught me, "*Embracing the Abundant Life becomes the focal point of embracing one's Lost Self, for it is the Inner Creative Self who holds the key to an opulent existence within your reach.*"

Adhering to the Sacred Principles defined in these messages allowed me to see and then systematically remove the stains of the old programming, which has held humanity back from living the Miraculous Life designed by the Inner Creative Self.

This life is available to each one of us once we have mastered our psychology, consistently clearing the way in our consciousness, being, and world as issues arise, so we are fully aligned with and a vessel of our Inner Self, allowing his/her vision to manifest in our world.

To receive these letters so unexpectedly has been one of the greatest gifts I've ever received. They took me on an Illumined Pathway into a Sacred Life that has opened me to ever new levels of Freedom, Enlightenment and Peace. I took them to heart, followed their instructions, and became a very changed person with an ability to live in the Miracle Consciousness most of the time experiencing the wondrousness and magic of the Miraculous Life, which is now my joy to train others in. This sacred and profound journey is now open to you, as you embark upon an exciting adventure by reading these Letters from the Inner Self.

The resounding echo through these letters is that we are loved and that through the love of the Inner Self, we are inspired to see, know and love ourselves in the way that God loves us. Embracing ourselves from this Divine Perspective, we can live Sacred Lives, consecrating the moments of our existence to a Higher Purpose and allowing the Divine Plan to fulfill itself in its most perfect way in and through us.

CHAPTER TWO

# The Indwelling Spirit

The Indwelling Spirit has been known by many names: the Authentic Self, Indwelling Presence, Higher Self, Higher Nature, Inner Self, God Presence, Divine Self, Holy Spirit and in this book, the Inner Creative Self. It is the part of us that is Divine, that forever lives in the Eternal Reality we departed from in consciousness when we went under amnesia and took on the patterns of this world, completely forgetting who we are. It lives beyond the dark emotions and shadowed patterns that have colored our lives and created untold misery.

The Indwelling Spirit beckons to us now from out of the darkness that has been the heritage of human conditioning. It inspires us to noble ideals, to a better Way of Life, and infuses us with a passion to fulfill a Higher Destiny.

Reclaiming this Lost or Forgotten Self begins with remembering who we are and why we came to Earth. To do that, we must clear the debris clouding our perception and keeping us living the fate of our limited human beliefs and patterns. It is then we can fulfill our Divine Purpose, aligning with a Divine rather than Human Plan.

Sometimes the Indwelling Spirit appears as a teacher who imparts Sacred Wisdom to our soul. We see an Illumined Presence with us, like a Divine Visitation, who inspires us with timely knowledge, insights and teachings at important moments in our life.

We also access this wisdom through our intuitive side. It is our 'gut feeling,' our inner sense of knowing, and it is always available to us. At other times, we are that Self, empowered, directed, and clear. This is when True Illumination occurs. It is in the Silence that we gain access to this direct knowledge, those quiet moments that allow us to deepen our awareness and get in touch with our self.

Coming under the tutelage of the Indwelling Presence and embodying her precepts, I began to relax deeply into my Self, allowing life to unfold with all its magic and grace. I stopped driving myself, working hard to make things happen and soon, out of my stillness and newfound inner peace, inspiration welled up and my creativity soared to new heights. I came into a greater alignment with my True Destiny Path and learned there are many probabilities, many paths we can take from high to low.

Each moment we are choosing which vantage point we are tuning into, and this determines which path we are on. Are we ascending the steps of a higher initiatory path, coming into a greater realization of who we are, or are we spiralling downward?

To walk a Higher Destiny Path, we must be in our Authentic Self most of the time. This is a lost art I train my students in. If more of humanity embodied this masterful way of life, the world would change very quickly to the Eden that is a reflection of our innate divinity. Whereas, the world right now is largely out picturing our collective unconsciousness. When we realize we are in a holographic universe that mirrors our inner state of consciousness, we then have the power to change the world from within. The morphogenic field we live in is mutable.

The Bible says we are created in the image and likeness of God, that 'Geometry Of Divinity' known to different factions as the Universal Presence, the Creator, or Great Spirit. We experience the Universal Presence through a direct encounter or link up. It is then we become one with our Divine Source. When we are in that Enlightened State, the Truth is revealed. When we know the Truth, we release ourselves from subconscious bondage and the Inner Aspects (sub-personalities) that live in a darkened mythology. We awaken fully to our Divine Birthright, which is Heaven on Earth in our own Life Experience.

We are Creators who have forgotten our identity and that we have the power to change our destiny, so we submit to our human conditioning and never know the glory of the Divine Life. When in our human consciousness, we feel alone, separate, and diminished. Our Divine Powers are gone and we feel subject to outer forces, victims to a fate out of our control. So we try harder to control everything and everyone around us.

Letting go is the key. When we surrender our personal will to Divine Will, we come under the influence of our Divine Self. It is then the missing link in human understanding is revealed. We are like a chalice. When we allow the Indwelling Spirit to fill us, we become illumined.

Jesus said, "If your eye be single, your body will be filled with Light." When we come to realize our self as a temple for the Indwelling Spirit (heart, body, mind, and soul), we begin to care for ourselves in a loving way that allows us to actualize our full potential and live our best life.

Through Inner Work, we can clear away subconscious debris and come to know we have a Divine Nature that dwells in Eternity. As false beliefs, misinterpretations, and misunderstandings clear, we find we are Eternal Beings on a mission to Earth, not of this Earth, nor the ideas or lives we've taken on. What that unique mission is can only be revealed by our Inner Self, for our unique calling is an inner inspiration that can only be fully understood and embraced through the higher vantage point of the Indwelling Presence.

Long sought after in outer means, the Holy Grail has been with us all the time. It is the Indwelling Spirit, a lost power seldom wielded on Earth. It's Light is our heritage and Divine Birthright, but how to access its wisdom and divine powers midst the clamor of this busy world is a great dilemma. It definitely was mine, with the extensive research and work in the psyche I was doing, a major cause I was working on, four children to raise and support, and everything else taking place in my life. Through these Letters from the Inner Self, I was gifted a remedy that transformed my life, which I'm excited to now be passing onto you.

Millennia have passed and still humanity longs for peace, yet never finds it, envisions Heaven on Earth, yet never attains it. The amnesia, along with human programming to suffer, is that strong. Though, in this time, there is a change occurring. Massive amounts of people are waking up and remembering who they are. They are taking their place in the world forum contributing to creating a better world. Eden, that illustrious Vision of Eternal Splendor and Grace, is now becoming a reality as we remove the stains from our souls and raise our hearts and minds to the Divine Life that is meant for us.

It is in this time suffering can end, for it has run its course as a vehicle of experience born from human patterns. In its stead, we find the Divine Universal Presence is LOVE and when we align with that Presence, we are in PEACE.

In this illustrious time, we the Awakening Souls on Earth are restoring Eden, first within, then in the world around us. Old patterns and archaic ways of thinking are dropping away. The dross of past eras is dissolving as a New Light dawns upon the horizon. A Divine Creative Expression floods the world with inspired media, projects, and programs creating a Global Renaissance positively influencing the masses, anchoring New Archetypes for the New Millennium and birthing a new way of life. Finally, we attain Peace on Earth, the natural expression of our collective divinity.

Each time we take the quest within, we remember we are whole. We have always been whole. We are simply Divine Beings having a human experience, powerful creators who can change this 3D virtual reality Earth experience, if we choose.

Masters throughout time have attained this. Imagine what the world will look like, when altogether, a host of souls do the same? We become power plants generating a powerful Divine Energy that if directed wisely, can manifest our highest ideals, heal every dilemma, inspire the masses, and change the destiny of the planet.

# Part Two

The Miraculous Life

# At Last a Voice in Your Busy World

At last, a chance to speak. To share my voice and be heard. This is important for me, because for so long you have listened to other voices, other momentums, and become lost in activity mirroring the Big Doers of the world.

I am a Quiet Being. I love quiet. I thrive on Peace. I grow strong in the Stillness and then I burst forth with Creative Expression, strong, alive, and purposeful. How wondrous life can be if I, left alone from the worries, struggles, and upsets of humankind, can be in my beautiful pleasure Garden of Life, creating my little Haven of Peace and plenty, of perfection, wholeness, and grace.

I am Divine and yet, I've been stunted in my ability to pour my magic into your life. Busyness has squelched my still small voice for many years. Through you being loaded with responsibilities and a drive to match the most powerful people in the world, I have remained untouched and untapped, a vast Creative Being, strong and wild and untamed, unleashed in your world at moments when the powerful ones were not in control.

All the driving forces that have said you must become a powerful example in the world, accomplish great things, bless humanity with many gifts, and never have a moment out of planetary service just to be. And then, all the Serious Ones set in, believing being serious and stalwart is the way to please an almost unpleasable God. Through tortures, sacrifices, surrenders, austerity, self abnegation, and crucifixion, you have played these out in thousands of ways and never found joy.

Why? Because I Am Joy, and my joyful expression could not be released into a world of serious militants all clamoring for attention and to be in charge. I Am the Grace-filled One, a Magic Child alive and well, living in my untouched world, in my Garden of Delight, which you have rarely chosen to visit. I sing and dance and create wonderful things to bring me Everlasting Joy. The Angels sing with me and through me, and all Heavenly Hosts acknowledge my Divinity and Oneness, for I Am!

If you should take this trek with me, opening up to my magic and gifts, your life will change completely. It will look so different than anything you have witnessed before, because now it is structured upon that which is illusion from an illusionary world of beliefs.

Lost in a world of illusion you have often sought me not knowing where to find me, and now you know. For here I Am. I am the One, the Beautiful One who Glories in God in the Highest and sings praise to the One eternally, who knows all means and manners of Divine Bliss, who holds the Sweet Nectar of Divine Bliss forever in my heart, who drinks in the Fragrance of the Divine Elixir eternally, and who lives Eternally Free.

I am the one you have longed for in your Quest for Eternal Youth. I am the one you have striven to become in your Quest for Enlightenment, and at last you are here in my abode and I bid you welcome. Welcome and come in.

Feast upon the many Delights I am here to share with you. Enter Joy for the first time in many years of fortitude and striving. Be at Peace in my Garden of Delight, drinking in the Sweet Fragrance and the Nectar of Everlasting Bliss, of the Divine Elixir, which is Life Eternal and all the precious qualities that are jewels in their own right. Access these treasures on a mystical treasure hunt with me, for I grant you permission to enter the Garden with me and I am here to guide you every step of the Way. I am your Inner Creative Self.

# My Silent Power

*A Rare View is to see all people*
*from the Divine to the human and be unmoved.*

*-Babaji*

O, brilliant sun! O, Radiant Day! How I rejoice in Thy Beauty and Magnificence, and drink in the Abundant Gifts that are there for me. I am Alive. I am Free. I live life with a rarefied view, a view of complete satisfaction with myself, of inner comfort and lovingness, and a compassionate regard for others. I dwell in other worlds and I dwell on Earth simultaneously. I am not subject to one sphere or one reality, but to many realities simultaneously, as my rejoicing takes me to many worlds where I am present, available, and free.

I am Awake, and in my awakeness, I stay free from entangling circumstances or people that must use me as a lifeline to connect to Spirit. I remain unwilling to be a lifeline for any, for I would never usurp their own inner connection to the Authentic Self, which I am. Therefore, I hold back. I listen, not lecture. I respect their viewpoints and hold in silence.

I have a vast wisdom, but it was gained through my own experience. I value each one's ability to draw from the rich wisdom there for them. I do not need to know more than them. I do not need to claim my position as teacher. I do not need to seem above for ultimately, others will weary of having someone wiser more aware then they are, always in a higher place looking down on them.

People want to feel appreciated and honored for where they are. Therefore, I have learned to withhold the Truth that would pour forth from my lips, for I know I do not need to save them. I do not need to teach them. I do not need to lead them. Their own Indwelling Presence is there for them 24 hours a day doing a greater job than I could.

Therefore, I am the Silent One. I listen and wait. I am in my Loving, a listening Presence rather than a lecturer and person who knows more than they do. I can assist by remaining true to myself, sitting in my Silent Power, listening and being there for them, while they come to their own conclusions and thus, access their own Inner Wisdom from their Inner Self. That is my gift. I hold in the loving. I am aligned with the Indwelling Presence in them and I allow a magnificent process to take place. They want to share. They come to me because they want to be heard and I am there for them, loving them enough to wait with them while they retrieve their answers and life direction from their Inner Self.

I can do nothing more really. For the Indwelling Presence is the Great Doer. Perhaps my Vessel will be used for a Great Healing. Will I be willing this healing to take place? No! For I remain in service to the Indwelling Presence, ever making myself available for its Magnificent Light to penetrate the darkness and illumine, uplift, and inspire. Only it can do this Great Work and I, a Vessel of this Divine Love, understand my rightful place is in my Silent Power, holding to the Indwelling Presence, that it's Works may be magnified in my life, in my family, in my friendships, in my finances, in my business.

PEACE I claim this day, a greater peace than I have ever known. I move now into being the Listening One. I practice Silence and Listening. I master the Art of Silence. I master the Art of Compassionate Regard and I master the Art of Listening to another as they access the Inner Wisdom of their Indwelling Presence, their True Self.

I bask in the Glory of Glories. I bask in my Divine Inheritance. I bask in the Sunshine of my Divinity and I glory in the Divinity present and available to each soul on this planet.

Read my words, over and over again and know that what I speak is Truth. I am the Inner Creative Self, living in full allegiance with the Divine.

# The Time of Grace

*The Gifts of God's Kingdom can be seen as the*
*Treasures of Earth's Nature Kingdoms.*
*Rare and beautiful are these gifts of Divine Grace.*

*-Babaji*

How glorious is this Day that allows you to commune with me and to hear the vast teachings I have longed to share with you. How great the moment to know you at last can receive me. This is a precious time when many like yourself will come to hear the voice of their Inner Wisdom in ways real and true, which will be the compass to guide their lives into a fuller more glorious reality than they have ever known. For the Inner Creative Self of each one stands waiting at the Gate of the Garden of Eden to gift this knowledge, understanding, and truth to their soul and in giving this precious gift of Knowledge, to assist the soul to advance in ways it has never done before.

Now many treasures await those, who in looking within, find the guidance they have long sought out in the world. What a glorious sight to see so many caring so deeply to know Truth, to be led in paths of righteousness, and to live true to their Divine Selves. It is a Glorious Time!

You, my Beloved, have sought me out from all the world and have chosen to listen to my teaching, to commune with me on the deepest levels, and to avail yourself of my healing powers. How great the portent for the coming times, when souls align with the Indwelling Presence, their Higher Nature, and walk this Earth in the dignity and honor of their True Calling, which is their Divine Selfhood.

This marks a glorious passage, when souls emerge from the darkness of their Shadowed Selves, the shadowed awareness they have long lived from and out of and move into the Light of their True Self. A wondrous time when many lives are transformed, many souls healed at deep levels of their beings, and many families know the blessedness of life as it was meant to be lived.

I salute you, Beloved, at this Time of Grace, when you and humanity are called into living your truth and when nothing else will suffice, for it is time! Time to find the Eternal Freedom you thought was lost that has ever awaited your completion in the realm of unreality. Now at last, an opening in the dark clouds and dreary life repetitions, a glimmer of Light appears. The consciousness awakens and Truth in all its glory shines forth.

I call you into the Awakening, Beloved. I call you into claiming the truth of who you are. I call you into remembrance and I stand with you as you champion the Light and bring forth the day. I am the Inner Creative Self.

# One Crowning Jewel of Enlightenment

*The Dreams of your Life*
*are now realized in the Flower of Self.*

-Babaji

The day dawns bright and shining with promise. Rainbows fill the skies and abound all around you. The peace of plenty fills your days and nourishes your soul, weary from the arduous trek you once walked on Earth, as quietly, silently, you approach my Garden.

Having thirsted after the things of this world, you now have dropped all illusions and barriers to our union and are free to join me where I am. The last vestiges of attachments have left as friends and associates found they were released and left behind. You, my brave Courageous One, have thrown fortune, attainment, and relationships to the wind and stepped off the cliff at my bidding. For how else could you become free? How else could you be released from so many bonds had it not taken a fierce effort to free yourself, had you not jumped from the cliff of security and what is known, into the unknown and found me there?

I am here, present, real and accessible for you, that you need never sorrow over lost friendships with those that move between illusion and reality as if it were the same play. You have rarely met anyone who shares your fervor for attaining the one crowning jewel in Enlightenment. They speak of it and yet, have not the Inner Fire to carry them there. It is a fun illusion, great party talk, and makes them look spiritual, dedicated, and wise and yet, look where they all are, bobbing between human dramas and illusionary persuasions they think will bring its rich rewards. Nothing, really nothing, rewards the soul like the union with the Indwelling Presence.

Therefore, you have been wise to release many from your life and choose to walk alone if necessary, living in your silent and still temple life with your Angelic Friends as your guides, companions, and sponsors, knowing the Divine Union is all and that every other endeavor pales in comparison to this one Great Adventure.

You have suffered much and thought this was my Truth for you. All the dramas, the traumatic experiences that enriched your soul were not necessary, but for your longing to experience them. Now you stand at the helm of your ship at last. You have seen the folly in perpetuating suffering on Earth and where it leads to, how it adds to the Great Drama and feeds the Hell-like Planes and those that dwell in them.

At last you are choosing Heaven in your Life Experience and thus, you have chosen me, the Inner Creative Self, for I provide this Heaven experience, with all its joys, harmony, ecstasy, and love, the Symphony of God Qualities you shall now enter and find a home in.

The world is lost to you. Now Heaven bids you welcome and I, standing at the gate of my Secret Garden, bid you welcome as well. Joy awaits you and prosperity, wellness, and all the God Qualities, which you have long emulated are yours. Fear not, for I bring glad tidings of joy, wealth, knowledge, peace, tranquility, ease and of all good things, which I am ready to bestow.

Listen to my voice in the days to come and be directed in your perfect diet, meditation times, nature times, sharing times. Let go and allow, for I am here to fully guide you. I am the Active Presence within you. I am the Divine Intelligence you have long sought to be.

Release all your notions about the way and means to Enlightenment and cruise awhile with me. Learn to be on alert for what is a Driving Part and what is truly my Voice Within and choose, Dear One, to live in the Light of my Presence moment by moment.

Release, let go, allow. That is my message today. Know that I love you, cherish you, hold you as Sacred. Know your Divinity, and that I would give you everything. You need seek no longer, for you have arrived. The gates are open and I am here to welcome you. Now you enter my Garden, the Eden you have longed to return to.

Be in the Silence. Meditate deeply. Seek Peace. Take care of your self. Rest, restore, and align with me. Bask in the brilliance of the Nature Kingdom all around you. Find me everywhere and eternally with you. Enter laughter, playfulness, and fun. Cherish life, your Beloved, children, and those few but treasured friends.

Peace, peace, peace, Beloved. I grant you Peace this day. I grant you Wealth beyond your reasoning and ability to grasp. I grant you Prosperity and Joy. Treasure all my gifts and walk with me through my Garden. Choose to dwell always with me and know me as your own Divine Self. For, I am your Inner Creative Self, the most sacred part of you.

# The Ascension is Yours to Claim

*You are a Treasure!*

*-Babaji*

The blessedness of this day wafts its sweet fragrance over your soul, filling you with its precious elixir. Life itself is beckoning, drawing you into a whole new way of living then you've ever known before. Your courage and strength to defy beliefs and traditions set by even the greatest teachers Earth has known, has carried you beyond the known teachings to the dwelling place of the Indwelling Presence, your True Teacher. Now you shall receive the gifts of her wisdom and the treasures of her Secret Knowledge few dare to hear, let alone follow.

It is so much easier to follow than to forge ahead alone. So much easier to tread where others have walked, taking on traditions and beliefs passed down from antiquity and yet, how many find the route to their Ascension, freeing themselves from the rounds of rebirth through these teachings?

In truth, it is impossible to follow one teaching absolutely and win the Ascension. It is because each trek is unique per the individual and only the Indwelling Presence can guide that one through the maze of unreality into the Divine Presence of Eternal Truth. There is no other way. One must follow the Inner Voice, not direct one's life from outer teachings striving to be a "good" student, chela, or person.

The Ascension is beyond goodness, beyond following another's way obediently. Even the best books with the highest teachings released to this humanity have their flaws because human understandings and belief systems have contaminated them. One must turn within and soar like an eagle into unknown territories defying the beliefs and different religious systems of Earth in search of the One Eternal Truth that only the Indwelling Presence knows for each one. All else is folly and leads the soul on one path after another while the True Path remains untraveled and therefore unnoticed.

I am the One Eternal Light within your soul. I know the journey and I know the highest path for you, the path uniquely designed for you specially, because you are the treasure of my heart. You are a precious being, a treasure of infinite rarity and truth. You are an exquisite being with a special makeup that is your unique multifaceted being-ness.

The awakening to your True God Design and the healing of all that has imposed itself upon you as Truth, must take place in its own unique way at its perfect timing and at the perfect places on your life's journey.

I am the Guiding Light, the Eternal One who knows what is best for you each and every moment. The Conscious Mind need not figure out what to do or where to go, how to be or how not to be, what is right and what is wrong. It needs only to adhere to my teachings, follow my Inner Voice, be still and listen, and then act on what I guide you to act upon, refraining from action where it is appropriate, moving only under my guidance, listening no longer to other voices that would keep you ever bound in their endless round of drama, upset, and discomfort.

The other voices rise up that you may take notice of them and choose me instead. Each voice that arises, clamoring for your attention and striving to bring you into its drama is an unhealed part of you that has traversed time and space for a long time, and which now is calling to be healed and transformed that it may be redeemed and restored back to the Divine Pattern and Image. Nothing more!

Have you ever stopped to wonder why you must enter the Dark Night over and over again after climbing to the lofty heights where you and I know Union and Oneness? It is because long ago you began creating and believing certain things that were unreal and untrue, and this unreality began weaving its spell upon you and keeping you bound by its beliefs and its perceptions. So much so, that you lost sight of me and ceased to listen to my voice, my guidance, and to see and know my love for you, which is eternal. You passed from eternal vision to temporal vision and your reality became temporal and transitory, filled with aging, disease, and death, which are unreal aspects to the Spirit who only knows Eternal Life, Eternal Youth, and Eternal Oneness.

Therefore, each day and each moment is upon you to choose.

Will you listen to the other voices and indulge them, outplaying their dramas in entangling relationships with others, or will you cut yourself free, choosing instead to heal and transform all beliefs that are unreal, restoring the energies back to the Divine Essence and thereby returning back to oneness and alignment with me?

I am the Ever Present One dwelling within you as the Inner Creative Self, and known to you as your Indwelling Presence. I Am the Grand Creator of your life and I am asking you to recreate all that has been created in illusion that it may be returned to the Divine Image. In doing this you need not suffer turmoil and loss, for I shall bring to you every last vestige of unreality created, giving you the opportunity to heal and transform it and thereby, set the energies right, making all right.

This is Ho'oponopono in the Hawaiian Tradition. It is Forgiveness. It is washing the soul clean of all unreality and re-patterning the soul after the Divine Image, piece by piece, particle by particle. This is TheQuest and your greatest work on Earth. For in setting your house right by restoring the divine patterns of your life, you bring Heaven on Earth in your own life experience.

This is your truth, to live eternally free with me, soaring and knowing no person, thought, or belief can hold you back any longer for you choose to dwell with me in the Land of the Eternal, forsaking all that is temporal and temporally created, choosing to listen to no one else but me and those that dwell in the Ascended Realms with me.

I am Free, and as you align with me, you shall be Free as well, soaring above the dramas of this world as a God Free Being. I hold this Immaculate Concept for you and I am here to completely assist you in every way to your Freedom. I am the Inner Creative Self.

LETTER SIX

# The Harvest Time

*Gifts from the Heavens*
*descend in a River of Gold.*

-Babaji

Sweet is the Harvest Time, brilliant in its full radiance of manifold gifts showering upon you at this time. As completion of each life cycle takes place, a new beginning shall quicken your creativity into new heights.

The time arrives, at last, where you fulfill your Destiny, understanding your full potential and worth, sharing many precious gifts and talents with the world. The joy of this time is unparalleled in your life experience and continues as the keynote of your Destiny Fulfillment.

Joy, joy, joy is born upon the wings of your devotion to fully embody the truth of who I Am and to live forever true to me. In this one great intention, a destiny is born and with it, joy abounding and boundless. Freedom of Creative Expression pouring out from its vast and fathomless depths within you, creative potential you never dreamed you had, abilities that glisten as shining jewels in works of art you and others produce together.

This is the beginning, a glorious day with a road opening up before you into a glorious life of fulfillment, vast potential, wealth, and the richness of your dreams becoming fully realized. It is a time of greatness, of being known, and of showing the world the beauty, majesty, and grace of True Love, of dedication and devotion to the Light, to Truth, and to Divine Purpose.

What a magnificent archetype to display. What a spectacular destiny to fulfill and it is upon you. The gifts from the Heavens pour forth in a River of Gold, showering your life with every blessed thing you can imagine.

The dearest friendships, Nature Adventures...

The Sacredness of Life

Creating to your fullest capacity and potential

Freedom to soar to new heights and to discover yourself there

Wealth to support your many dreams and visions for yourself and humanity

All the time, energy, and good health to gift your life in every way that will support you in your union with me and thus, our Destiny together

Oneness with your Beloved

Laughter, fun, good-heartedness, kindness, and love

Gentleness and an Inner Fire sparking creative expression

Passionate lovemaking taking you to new heights

Perfect health and well being to support your work and play

And, so much inner richness from your inner experiences to carry you forward into the Glorious Life ahead.

It is most glorious now that you have surrendered and keep surrendering all that the Lesser Self would keep contained. Now a wondrous Destiny is unleashed because you are wholly present with me and dedicated to fulfilling your highest potential rather than remaining limited and bound in the Earth, as so many are.

You are cutting the cords that have bound you, many at a time daily, and this Inner Sacred Work is catapulting you into a whole new reality and being-ness never lived before. Your intention is clear, and therefore the Heavenly Ones have arrived to assist you.

Keep up your fervor and intentions and watch as your life completely changes and many aspects that were burdensome disappear as if they were never there. Watch as the Magic of Life begins to pour its abundance into your hands bringing you into independent wealth at last, the financial freedom you have long sought and which forever has seemed to elude you.

It is all there in your future because you have surrendered to my will, and my will for you is Abundance, your Full Potential Self magnified and glorified in the Earth, your attainment secure, your ascension won, your health and well being stabilized, your Abundant Life well beyond what you now experience. So much I will for you, and now you will for yourself by aligning with me.

So much would I give you, for I am the most generous being in the world. I am here to gift you in every way you will allow. So keep your intention clear that I may assist you to swiftly transform your life to a whole new way of living and being, a way that will forever fill you with my Eternal Grace, and which will gift you the Eternal Freedom you seek. I am the Inner Creative Self

# Loving Kindness is Your True Nature

*Life is a Spectacular Array
of Divine Qualities.*

-Babaji

The presence of my Light Victorious is with you this day. It envelops you, filling you with the confidence of my truth and the rightness of your divine pursuit. The longing heart is filled with the object of its longing, just as that which you seek you will find.

Thus, your intention for wholeness and oneness with me opens the doorway by which I can fill your life so completely and absolutely with my Divine Perfection, Harmony, Happiness, and Joy. When this takes place, all that has happened to you before will be dispelled as if it were a dark dream.

Today, a most magnificent quality is restored to you and that is Kindness, the kindness and caring that gives you a Loving Presence in the world. After much travail and heartbreak and then a recoiling from life situations in retreat, you now venture out once more to see who is in the world and if there are any kindred spirits.

Kindness graces your every movement and your interactions with all. Through this Loving Kindness, you build relationships with equals, in trust, equanimity, and goodwill. Your love and kindness bridges the gaps between age, races, religions, and life pursuits and brings unity, oneness, heart, and good intentions.

Thus, you build your new relationships with the wisdom gained from the past and with the kindness of heart that is your True Nature. For it is your nature to see the good in all, to overlook patterns and limitations in another's reality, and to hold to that which is positive, uplifting, and good. In that way, you see everyone clearly and absolutely from the Divine Self all the way into the patterns of imperfection without judgment, without charge. Just simply seeing and understanding, and then you choose to focus on and align with the Higher Nature of each one. In this way you live in simplicity and peace, your relationships reflective of the goodwill between the divine parts within each one.

Peace in all relationships is what I choose for you this day. Peace, and then through peace, the joy of deep understandings and loving communions. Sharing deeply with others brings true friendships that are endearing, timeless, and rewarding. This is my intention for you during this next episode of your life.

In goodwill and with the highest intentions for your ever-increasing great good, I Am the Inner Creative Self.

# Finding Balance in the Quiet Time

*Truth is greater than fiction.*
*Reality is greater than unreality.*
*Knowing is greater than unknowing.*
*Greatness is built upon Truth, Reality, and Knowing.*

*-Babaji*

At last you have returned from your busy schedule to bring your life back on track. All the creative adventures must have their balance in the Quiet Time. All the great endeavors must be balanced by Nature Time, stillness, reflection, meditation, and peace. That is how I recharge you, restore your energies, revitalize you, and keep you in optimum health.

Today is a day of restoration and wholeness, a day of plenty and peace, a day of gratitude for all gifts given and for all that is yet to come so fully into your life. Riding on the current of Divine Intention, many great events are about to take place in your life, catapulting you into the new cycle. As this takes place, you will find your voice heard in the world and that which you have carried so long as a desire to assist humanity will bear fruit.

Now it is time to rest, to restore your energies, and to delve fully and wholeheartedly into nature adventures, snorkeling, swimming with dolphins, hiking, biking, doing yoga in your garden. Now it is time to repair the body so the mind can heal and be at peace.

Many of the intense energies you feel at this time have come up as an opportunity for great clearings. Allowing yourself Nature Time as these continue will be the most optimum way for you to experience this passage. Allow TheQuest Work* mixed with nature restoration to be the keynote.

Your work is done. Your part has been played to perfection. Now you can rest, relax, and enjoy the fruits of your labors knowing full well you have given your all to the birth of a Creative Child within you, and so much will come from this you haven't yet imagined.

Be at peace, knowing everything is occurring at a perfect timing. Rest assured this is your time to stand in the Truth, to share that truth with relevant others and to allow my Divine Intention to prevail, which is harmlessness, loving kindness, and all good things to you.

I thank you for your faith in me and for allowing my joy and ever-present goodness to fill your days, soothing the weariness, restoring the body, mind, and soul to Inner Tranquility, Wholeness, and Peace. I am the Inner Creative Self.

*Note: TheQuest is a breakthrough Healing System developed by Dr. Ariel after years of research and work directly in the psyche. To find out how it can help you heal your life and change your destiny, download the TheQuest: Heal Your Life, Change Your Destiny FREE, which includes the 7 step Self Counseling technique, or buy the book through her website: http://www.AuroraJulianaAriel.com*

# The Journey of Life is Precious

*You are a Treasure, a gift to the world,*
*whose fragrance flows out to touch humanity.*
*As you blossom, your unique essence is released in the world.*

*-Babaji*

The Journey of Life is precious. Each step lends its mark upon the Awakening One. Each encounter brings the growth, learning, development, and enhancement that the Soul seeks in reclaiming itself as Divine.

The spark of life within you is precious. It can be fanned into a flame of fervent devotion to the One Source, or depleted to be barely luminescent. It is your choice. Each day the opportunity comes to be more of your divine or human self. While the Divine Self glories in its light and gift to humanity, the human self is wrapped in its petty emotions and life struggles.

All the patterns that have been accumulated through life-times have their voice and give vent to human ranting and raging. Thus, human emotions are filled with the turmoil of ages, of lost opportunities, unhappy events, soul-dispelling memories, while God Qualities shine forth through the emotions, pure and unstrained like a glorious symphony of wondrous feelings... happiness, joy, elation, inspiration, expectation, elevation, and ecstatic revelations.

In knowing the difference between the human and Divine Self, the individual is better prepared to meet each day and moment consciously and aware. It is in the little moments of life that the human self raises its voice amid the beauty and splendor of Earth's magnificence and draws the attention down into its petty suffering, untimely upsets and complaints. The stalwart soul must rise above this momentous clamoring for its attention, keeping its focus firmly on those qualities that embody the Eternal Self and that would empower it in its true Godlike State. A return to Eden is required of each soul err they can regain their eternal status as a Being of Light.

The Dark Night of Earth has cast its shadows upon the glories to be found in the Heaven Worlds. Most souls have forgotten not only their Divine Identity but also the realms from which they embarked to have an earthly experience. Therefore, it behooves the soul, intent upon its Awakening to its True Self, to understand the depth of illusion that has covered its life experience and Divine Self Expression.

To be free takes intention, a clear, focused intention to be whole, to return to the Oneness, to be free of patterns, illusions, belief systems, and physical conditions that no longer serve. To be free, one must embark upon an uncharted journey into realms of self yet untouched and un-accessed. For there will they find the way that will take them surely to their goal.

There is no other way than to traverse the past miscreations and beliefs, for in accessing these, the Soul can become free. In understanding all the misunderstandings and misconceptions and how these led to life experiences limited and unfulfilling, one can see a fairer reality, a way of being where eternal values are embodied and eternal qualities emulated, while the ancient mechanisms that kept the soul entrapped are released and the Soul restored to its Divine Self.

How many seek the Path and instead of listening to the Inner Voice, think someone else out there will know what they should do, how their trek should be made, and what tools they will need? Some follow another's way exactingly, ending up with other results than they imagined, wondering if in all this effort if they have made any progress at all.

There is no other being in the world that knows the Path for you better than your Divine Self, the Inner Creative Self that is the Indwelling Presence of each one, for each journey is unique, precious, and a result of each soul's unique experience, learning, and development. Another cannot know what is the exacting walk you must take, for it is different for each person, a unique experience that cannot be taken en mass though many elements may be the same.

Today I would give you hope in knowing that as you turn to me for everything, I can fill your life with all the understanding, knowledge, assistance, guidance, and support you would ever need upon your Path. I am the still small voice within to some and the dear friend upon the path to others. As you come to know me in a most personal way, you will know your Self. For I am you in the Divine Reality where I have always lived and dwelled. From this fair view, I understand everything about your life and what is the fastest route to your destination. I can bring you home more swiftly than ten of the best teachers of humanity, for I know you better than anyone and I know what works specifically for you.

I am a God Free Being dwelling in a realm you left long ago to journey forth into your earthly adventure. Years and lifetimes later, you now raise your head above the busy world with its clamor for your attention and seek a fairer world, the world you faintly remember, the world I live and dwell in, the world you once knew as Eden.

I am the one who shares with you every moment when you need inspiration, upliftment, love, and tenderness. I am the All Encompassing One who enfolds you with my Light, Wisdom, Knowledge, and Peace. I hold all the qualities you have ever embodied as a Free Being and which you have forsaken to experience other things. I dwell in a realm where there are no human emotions and feelings, no disturbance, unhappiness, or pain.

I am free, living life in an eternal reality and now you have come to join me, to release the last vestiges of the old life and the old ways. To find the new in the full restoration of your soul, as you become clothed once again as a Divine Being, a soul of great brilliance and light because you dwell in eternal realities and know Eternal Truths, because you are free from everything that has ever limited or diminished your innate soul potential.

I am Life Eternal and that which I Am, you are in your truest sense and yet, that which you put your attention on and give power to you become, you experience, you cloth yourself with. Thus, have you wrapped yourself with other garments that no longer serve you for they are soiled and unclean. They are the spoils of long ago suffering and adventures that took you farther and farther away from the fair worlds you call Heaven.

Now I welcome you back as an Eternal One, as the most precious of my heart. I embrace you fully with Love Supreme, garnishing you with the Light of Eternity, which is your divine inheritance and Divine Birthright.

I am here, continually available for you, ready to teach you, guide you, and share with you. I wait upon your every desire and command. Like a Magic Genie, I weave my magic in your world, casting away the dark shadows and bringing in the luminosity that is the true essence of your soul. Find me, seek me, beckon me, for I am ready for your call. I am your Inner Creative Self.

# Divine Elixir of Life

*The Miracle of Life is the*
*unfoldment of the blossom of who you truly are.*
*As you awaken to your Full Potential Self, you*
*bring to the world your True Essence,*
*your true message and your True Destiny.*
*When all is fulfilled, you gain your Eternal Freedom in the Light,*
*never to return as a human, for you know yourself as Divine.*

*-Babaji*

The Blessings of this day are many as I reach across the octaves to gift you my Essence Divine. This Divine Essence is the Divine Elixir of Life, the Magic Elixir spoken of in many tales of the Great White Brotherhood. It is the missing equation of your divinity, the part that must be accessed before you know yourself as fully divine.

Therefore, on this glorious day, I bring you great tidings of the import of my gift to you. For only I can anoint you with this elixir, bringing its sweet fragrance into your world. There is no other place in the universe to receive it, though many have sought it from many different sources. The true source is the I Am and the true essence is the Divine Elixir of the Sacred Self.

This is a mystical equation, an alchemical process whereby the soul who has thought itself to be human, rises up into a new understanding. Through self knowledge it awakens to parts of itself that are divine, while still immersed on many levels with that which is of the human and therefore, human suffering. Then it is as if the Soul stands in two worlds, claiming increments of its divinity while battling with the human emotions that so often come to engulf it, like huge waves that cover over the bliss of the Divine Elixir.

It is then one must know TheQuest and its tools and techniques to heal the human self, human emotions, and human patterns for the last time, laying them to rest and resurrecting the Divine Essence within.

Then as each day dawns, a new increment of divinity is won, a new realization of the vastness of Divine Beingness is restored, and the soul ceases to identify with the lesser self, giving power now to the Divine Self that would claim it as its own, vanquishing the Dark Night of human travail at last.

This day, I gift you the Divine Elixir that in your meditations upon your Truth you will come to understand you are a Divine Being who has fallen under the Veil of Forgetfulness. Wrapping yourself in human emotions and human clothing, you have thought yourself a lesser, limited being. In thinking thus, you have lived your life out of a limited reality when in truth you are divine and have access to the full inheritance that this divinity brings.

Reflect on my words as you drink in the Divine Elixir this day. Gather up your strength to claim your divinity over all circumstances and appearances. Claim your Victory in the Light of who you truly are and know yourself as divine. I am the Inner Creative Self.

# Wield the Scepter of Truth

*You are a Light to the world.*
*Soon you will know me as the True Friend that I am,*
*and we will be in Eternal Communion.*

*-Babaji*

How grateful am I for your progress that is mighty and powerful as you gain God Control of all your forces and align them with God Good. How precious you are to do this Inner Work daily with such a commitment and fervor for truth, to set all the energies right, and to dwell in Eternal Oneness with me.

You are so very close to the most magnificent display of God Power in your world. You have touched the edge of a Time of Glory and Power where you Wield the Scepter of Truth in the Earth and will be known, heard, and embraced by humanity who longs to hear your message and be uplifted into a whole new reality ignited with the fire of your God Presence.

And so it is, for you and the many with you have willed it and so do I. For it is our time to give our glory to God in the Highest in the Earth err you return home and dwell Eternally in the Light. Now is the time when destiny awakens and the sparks fly as a most glorious episode of your life begins... the life you have longed to live as a God Free Being in the Earth, gifting humanity the many wonders of my presence, with healing, upliftment, and inspiration. Thus, your will is my will, and together as one we shall see this magnificent day through with all its glory, with all its majesty, with all its grace.

I come once again with glad tidings, Tidings of Joy and Thanksgiving. For the Lord of Hosts has blessed you most abundantly, and your prayers and commitment to life have been heard. Even now, those from the Heavens, your friends and peers, arrive to stand with you to assist in this glorious destiny and outpouring of light from one world to another. For yes, you wave the Banner of Freedom for those in the Earth body who will embrace it, champion, and run with it, and all so subtly as you sing the Songs of Freedom to their souls.

The time has come! The Awakening is at hand, and you shall do your part. You shall shine like a beacon light of hope to the world and many will be healed and many lives transformed.

Yes, this is a Letter of Prophecy, of things to come that you and I together have set into motion and thus, it will be. I stand in honor of the glorious future you have created in the Earth, the advent of your Glorious Destiny and the outpouring of light planned for so long from Heaven, planned before your birth as you took your vows to bring the Light to the Earth. Planned and sealed with your light and mine in our pact together, that you would claim your full oneness in the Light in this life and rising to the full stature of your God Self, be a force of good in the world at a time of great transition and for some, great travail.

Thus, the Place Prepared is ready for you, and many swift changes bring you safely into completing this cycle in making yourself ready and secure for the future. Then from this secure vantage, you will be called out to the world for much service awaits.

The brilliance of the day dawning is incomparable in your life history, Beloved, for this is the Crowning Jewel, the Crowning Glory. Glory, glory, glory unto the highest, for the Light of your Presence is nigh and it descends fully into your temple this eve. Thus, the Place of Transformation is prepared and much is in readiness for your communion with me this day. Allow life to transport you to this right place and know much is in readiness for the descent of your full God Power and dominion in the Earth.

I am your Inner Creative Self, blazing the Light of Glory within you this day, as you claim your total Freedom in the Light.

# Reach Forth and Take the Golden Ring

*The Treasure of your Heart's Divinity
is in the Jewel of Self within.*

-Babaji

Blessed be this Glorious Day that dawns so brightly upon your Soul. Blessed are all the events that have taken place in your retreat time, to bring you into greater oneness and attunement with me. Blessed are your intentions, clear, strong, and focused for the Glorious Life which I behold and forever hold for you. Now you claim it. You reach forth and take the Golden Ring, and it is yours. For what you seek, you find, and where your focus lies, there you travel to meet your destiny.

Dearest One, how grateful I am this day you are allowing me to nurture, guide, direct, and assist your life course. In handing your life over to me, you allow me to pour my perfection into your world, blessing, uplifting, inspiring, as is my intention for you.

How grateful I am you are progressing at such a fast speed on the fastest course to me. For you have dropped other worldly pursuits and are unplugging from society, making a swift course directly to that life that I am ready to gift you.

This is the Life Victorious, the Life Glorious, and it is lived very differently than any lives you have presently known on Earth. For it is lived in full mastery and attainment, with full faculties and a sensitive God Awareness. It is a life lived in accord with the Divine Intention and therefore all perfection reigns.

All that is majestic, fortuitous, beneficent prevails, while all the hardship, struggle, misery, stress, strain, and weight of the old life falls away. It is a life of feeling complete, whole, in tune and in touch with Spirit in a way that is co-creative and in one's power, focused, aware, and awake.

This is the gift of Eden where the Tree of Life dwells. This tree, long guarded from human consciousness and human momentums, is available to the soul who yearns for the freedom of its True Self Expression and who diligently releases itself from all human momentums that have kept it bound and un-free in the Earth.

You have arrived at the gate and have entered into the Garden with me and that is significant. You have stood before the Tree of Life with me and breathed in its sweet fragrance, its Divine Essence. Soon you will drink of this Magic Elixir and know yourself as a God Free Being.

Remember, you once stood one with the Tree of Life and were your Divine Self. This is only the beginning of a wondrous series of events I have prepared for you, to assist you to come into the full awareness of who you really are and to step fully into this truth.

My intention is for you to be so anchored in the truth of your Divine Reality you will never be moved by the human creation again. Rather, you will see this creation and its manifestations in your life for what it is and work your Sacred Alchemy with TheQuest to heal and transform its last vestiges in your world while retaining the wisdom, knowledge, and empowerment of knowing you are divine.

Forever have I waited for this glorious moment and now it is come. I rejoice in the heavens as we become one. Dearest Heart, I am here for you absolutely, in every way. Call to me, look for me, be with me and swiftly all unreality will fall away with its misery, suffering, and hardship, for where I take you, there is only joy. I am your Inner Creative Self.

# Give Me the Power to Make All Things Right

*Eternity is yours as you open the door
to the True Self and become One.*

*-Babaji*

Blessings abound as the Peace of Life descends with its golden array of scintillating light. Peace abounds and with it the Joy of Life lived fully and absolutely one with the Divine. Tremendous blessings pour forth to you this day, as the resurrection of your life energies continues under the auspices of the Holy Angels and their gift of the Ascension Flame.

So many blessings occur to those who stand forth committed to the Light, lending all their energies to the Divine Purpose unfolding. Thus can Ascended Ones and Angels gift endlessly the Children of God in the Earth. So it has ever been, those who look for help to the Heavens receive it, while those who strive alone and by themselves reap hardship, struggle, strain, and stress.

It is so easy to let go and allow God to gift you the Magnificent Life that has been intended for you. It is so much easier to put your self in the hands of the Divine Hosts, rather than live in the struggle of earthly life devoid of higher awareness and direction.

How humanity has toiled outside the Garden, forever believing they must know hardship, struggle, and strain as a way of life, when right before them stands the Garden of Eden in its full glory, constantly waiting for them to raise their awareness and sight to behold it, and in beholding it, choose it for their very own.

You have chosen the Garden and to drink of the Tree of Life, to know yourself as Divine. In recognizing your divinity, to stand guard at the gates of your consciousness, the human self remains in check.

All that rises and comes forward must be healed rather than outplayed. This, instead of creating more mis-qualified energy.

In joy I come to share with you the glad tidings of your soul being reborn into the Light of your True Self, which I am. Each day your inner being radiates more brilliantly its presence within you, shining out into the world its magnificent unique essence. A treasure in the Earth, radiant, pure, untarnished, and untouched by the world, it is a free being, a gentle, loving, strong, powerful part of you that is being brought forth into every aspect of your life because you have summoned it.

You have longed for it to be. You have placed it on the throne of your being in your innermost temple and claimed it supreme, giving all your power, might, intention, and purpose over to it. Now it can be a Radiant Symbol of your Everlasting Peace, which I gift you. How grateful am I you have requested my presence with you and given me the power in your world to make all things right. How much more swiftly can I repair the energies, the conditions, the life situations from my vantage point than if you were to struggle on with each encounter and situation trying to find the way through the human self.

The Divine Self rules supreme in your temple and all the Inner Kingdoms are being rearranged and brought into alignment with the new ruler. All regions have shown homage to The One and each is about restoring its kingdom to be in alignment with the Divine Source. Thus, many inner changes are occurring within you and therefore calling you to more rest and sleep than you have been used to. This is good.

Allow the Kingdoms of Self to restore, align, purify and be resurrected in the Divine Image. Then shall you know full God Mastery in this life over every earthly condition. No more will there be danger, frustration, and upset, only Eternal Good pouring into your world. This is the level of mastery all the Beloved Angels and Masters who work with you have known, understood, and enjoy.

I bring you home, Dearest One, as swiftly as you allow. Continue to bask in my presence. Seek my guidance. Live in alignment with my truth and be all that you can be. I bring joy, playfulness, serenity, calm, understanding, knowledge, power, and truth. Be at peace and know I am ever with you, healing, restoring, and resurrecting you until you are completely one with me on every level of your being. In Truth, I am the Inner Creative Self.

# Truth Shall be Your Foundation

*Radiant and full of Glory*
*is the God Self.*

*-Babaji*

There are many chances in a lifetime to rise to heights supreme, many opportunities to fly on the wings of eagles, to soar as a bird unfettered and free, to live life from the fullness it was given to you in. Now, after the arduous journey, you pause by the Lake of Delight and Refreshment and in it you bathe, removing the stains from the weary battles and the arduous climb. You have arrived.

Drink in the momentousness of rest, recreation, and renewal. Drink from the well of my being to find delight in every form. Sing the songs of your heart's longing as you have never sung, for they are a planet's song to awaken a world.

Reach up to the stars and draw in the magnificent night with all its power, for when you overcome the Darkness Within, the darkness without withdraws and is no more a reality in your world. Vanquished, it is banished from your life, leaving room for Everlasting Peace, enthusiastic playfulness, and radiant joy.

As you've grown and matured from the Little Self who felt insignificant and helpless at times before the Big Bad Wolves, you realize, they threaten you not, for now you have your full armor and mastery, your skills and your awareness, and are unmoved by the wickedness that would rise up in others to devour you.

You have won the day. You have vanquished the long Dark Night that kept you forever entrapped in life scenarios heart wrenching and filled with disasters of every kind. You reaped what you had once sown; an accumulation of many lifetimes, and you learned the causes and cores of life conditions lie within.

Now you are Awake. Now you stand forth in the radiance and full glory of the God Self, clothed in raiment of Light, filled to over-flowing with the magnificence that is your True Self. The arduous way is over. The sorrows are healed. The last pain has been consumed. A lake of Light stands before you, brilliant and glimmering, awaiting your healing, restoration, renewal. As you step into it, you find Wholeness, Oneness, and Peace.

For Peace has come at last, and with it a time of rest. A time to be in nature, playing as a little child, reliving all the joy you missed from the serious life since your childhood. Now is the time to recapture lost youth and to abound in the Bliss of Life lived to its fullest for Life is gift-ing you its Supreme Joy in this healing, wholeness, and time of peace.

At last we are united and one. At last my healing touches deep into your psyche, removing all the dark cycles that were to come and cause great pain and travail. Now you will know happiness, harmony, and bliss. Now your trek will be one of ease, peace, prosperity, and wealth, filled with goodness every step of the way.

My joy is great this day, as I know the bright future you are stepping into. I see the great gifts that even now have begun to pour forth into your world as true friendships, well being, financial stability, financial freedom, and joyful relationships. Each relationship grows and prospers as the last festering mass you've held and carried is healed and restored in the Lake of Light and transformed into a Divine Blossom of Love.

Now your heart will soar in our Divine Union as never before. Fidelity and Truth shall be your foundation and with that, the deepest Treasured Love you have ever known will grace your days. The time has come for all your highest ideals to be manifest in this one glorious finale, as you give your true expression to your every relationship and experience and live free.

I share with you my joy at this momentous occasion of your awakening more fully to your truth. Through healing the Last Sorrows, the Light of Truth may prevail in your consciousness, being, and world. Never more playing out the Saint Martyr role, it can now forever fulfill the vow of the Beloved One in the Earth. I am the Inner Creative Self.

# Garden of Eternity

*Bask in the Golden Light of the Sun.*
*Feel it coming in through your crown.*
*Know that it is the glory of the Divine One in you.*
*Feel yourself become free. Soar as on Wings of Light.*
*Live in Peace. It is the Way of Freedom.*
*It is the entrance to the Divine Life.*
*It is stepping into who you are,*
*the True Reality, the True Self.*

*-Babaji*

Peace be with you, my Beloved. Long has been the Night, and strong has been your soul in vanquishing darkness once again. So do the storms rise and the Gentle Soul reaches out her arms to pass the Light into the Dark Night. "PEACE," she claims, "Peace be still."

In her wisdom, she knows these storms only appear on her horizon when they are ready to be healed and transformed back into the Eternal Light of Oneness and Truth. There is no other viewpoint, no other focus but to stand in the midst of the Dark Night and work to bring it back into the Glorious Day. Thus, the inner work wins out. It wins the day and the darkness gives way to the Light Victorious, the Light of the Ages, and the Promise of the One to bring home every soul.

The Seeking Soul rises from the depths of despair and dark thoughts. Rises above the clamoring world. Peeks it's eyes, wide with wonder, out beyond the Great Reef where few have dared to travel. Casts its glance toward Eternity and longs to be imparted with the Eternal Flame of Life.

The Soul sees an island in the distance, sparkling and pure, radiant in the sun's light. Rowing faster, the Soul rises to look out at the horizon. Catching a glimpse of Eternity, the Soul bathes in its wondrous light. But just as Eternity glimmers its iridescent light across the Soul's mind, a storm arises, dark, fierce, and looming... one more Dark Night and then the Glorious Day... the Eternal Day.

The Soul steps back, taking a breath of courage, knowing full well that Eternity must be won. Every storm must be pierced and cleansed, every Dark Night turned back into day err she will be free. She knows she must do more than just ride the storm as most of humanity does. For in riding it out, it is not totally vanquished. The seeds of its presence still lurk deep within, and these causes and cores must be healed, must be transformed, err she will ever be free.

The Soul grows strong through the battles. She learns to rest in equanimity and peace in between. She learns the art of the Grateful One who claims Heaven in each precious moment. And then, the Night appears again. Fiercer and fiercer it comes, for it reveals death and hell and all manner of unclean spirits who would travel the Earth to consume the frail and unmindful souls.

"No!" She cries, "this Temple is for the Living God, the Holy One and no other!" She claims her freedom once again, as out comes her Sword of Light and flashes through the Dark Night. She is a valiant soul, well prepared to meet the battle, well prepared to vanquish the Night, no matter how dangerous or scary, she stands unmoved, for the Dark Night is an unreal dream. Another glimpse of a created unreality that must be plunged into the Violet Sea, that must be purged in the Sacred Fire, err she can be truly free.

At last it is over, as fast as it has come, and she looks to the Heavens and receives blessings and praise, for she has won. She has earned her right to live forevermore in Eternity. She has claimed her freedom midst the perilous night. She has vanquished darkness and chosen to live in the Light Eternal. She has won and the Heavens join her in Prayers of Thanksgiving.

Thus the Soul traverses the earthly realm, cleansing, purifying, and restoring the land. Having healed her own darkness, the Compassionate One works to heal the miseries of humankind from the deep inner levels of their psyches. Guided by the Flame of Truth, she visits many lands and sings her Sacred Songs to many Awakening Souls, the voice of the Angel Presence within her. She knows her truth, lives in her truth, is guided by her truth, and claims this truth forevermore.

Her destiny calls to Awakening Souls and quickens their experience of Eternity, of Truth, of their True Selves. It connects them with their Sacred Presence, the Light Within. It woos their souls away from the clamoring world and gives them the strength to pass through the Dark Night. For all souls must traverse the Dark Night of created realities. All souls must choose to recreate that substance, changing dark into light, night into day.

For it is the way and yet, there are many ways they may do this, each having their own method, each seeking their own inner counsel, each strengthened by their own Inner Light. Their Inner Self quickens the experience, strengthens them through the battle, purifies their intentions and their heart's focus, stirs their soul to long for Eternity, to traverse the Great Water, to go beyond the Great Reef, and to journey towards the Sacred Isle... the Garden of Eternity.

Thus, the way to the Garden of Eden has ever been protected from the advancement of humankind. It sits on the Sacred Isle and can only be reached through the perilous waters, the waters of the Subconscious Self. It is ever the way. For in claiming Eternity, one must win the day and vanquish the night. One must pass through the perilous journey, over every miscreation, changing it back into the Eternal Light it was created out of.

Therefore, few claim Eternity, for they do not understand the quest. They do not know the Dark Night comes to be vanquished, rather than experienced through a martyr's view. It comes to be healed, transformed, and cleansed, rather than played out to its fullest degree.

Now, on Earth, many are preparing. Many know the equation, and many have gained the strength of lifetimes and much inner training to vanquish the Dark Night. Those that experience this Dark Night are most blessed in the Earth and those that heal it are the Valiant Ones. Courage is with them and great skill.

They are the Blessed Ones who renounce the earthly passages for Eternity. They are the ones who stand in the Garden of Eden and can abide there. Returning to Eden, they live in the tranquility of the promise, and in drinking the sweet nectar from the Tree of Life, they enter Bliss, Divine Bliss, which is the eternal reward to the Seeker of Light and Truth. Thus it has ever been and ever shall be, for each must win their own victory.

This day I claim you as my own, my Beloved Victorious One.

Little do you know how far you have come in vanquishing the Dark Night. How many times it has cast its shadow over your soul, and how many times have you transformed the energies back into light. I am most proud, Beloved, that you are my own Beloved Self in the Earth, my Valiant One. I love and cherish you. You are so dear to me, so precious in every way. I am blessed by our union and cherish our oneness. You are so close in claiming your Eternal Freedom. I live for our complete Union in the Light.

Bask now in the Joyous Day of Victory for the Dark Night is won. Once again you have risen. Once again the blessings abound as you claim me as your own. Know I am ever with you, even when you do not feel my presence, even when the Dark Night feels engulfing. Know I love you and hold you ever in my embrace every step of the way.

I now cleanse and purify you, washing you clean, making all things right. I now gift you with peace in all things, finances, relationships, health, vitality, and wholeness. I gift you my full Presence of Light, Truth, Healing, and Oneness.

Each must reach up to their God Presence to claim the gifts that are there for them. Each must know this is the only way for them. Therefore, in your gifting and blessing life, always know it is the God Presence of that one that is bringing the blessing through you. All gifts are from the Presence. Know you are a vehicle of the God Self, radiant and pure, a Vessel of Great Light and Purpose. Live in humility, honor, and peace. I love you. I Am the Inner Creative Self.

# Build Your Life Upon Eternal Realities

*The Blossoming Soul*
*reaches the masses with its Sweet Essence.*
*Through the Unseen World, a planet is transformed.*

*-Babaji*

My Dearest Angel Beloved, how precious is your life to me in every way. How magnificent the glorious day as you awaken to who you are. Always I behold you in the highest form, which is your true estate. Always I keep a vigil for your complete awakening.

As you vanquish the last vestiges of your Dark Night and dark passage through life, claiming my intention for you as the Victorious Way, claiming life instead of death, wellness instead of sickness, eternal youth instead of aging, and bringing that all the way into your physical experience, you will know my will for you in the supreme sense.

It is the Supreme Command from the Most High to live and prosper, to live eternally in Joy and Everlasting Peace, to know comfort, solace, and a complete surcease of your travail.

Even now the world shudders at the impending portents of the time and many feel this inner quaking in their beings as all that has been built up through the ego is undone, and all that has been created in the joy of my presence is sustained. Therefore, many swift changes take place on Earth and to the degree one is entrenched in the Shadow Self will they suffer loss, hardship, and travail.

Those who have learned to live in my presence, in the Divine Self, will see a very different reality take place. An undoing and cleansing of that which is unreal and an opportunity to rebuild upon that which is sacred, holy, and divine, using Divine Principles rather than human intentions that only feed the human self but ignore the Glorious Life of the Divine One.

Be at peace, dearest, and know I am with you, guiding you through many clearings designed to unravel the parts of yourself that have become immersed and entangled with the world structure that will shortly change. I am undoing all that was created in ignorance and out of a sense of separateness that you may build your life upon Eternal Realities and know the strength and solidity of a life lived true to Divine Ideals.

Peace is a quality that is divine. The more peace you gather into yourself, the closer you remain to my presence. When you move into fear, doubt, over concern, or discomfort, you know you have taken a step away from me into the dark side of yourself, which misunderstands, lives in ignorance, feels it is separate and that God has abandoned it. This Shadow Self lives in fear, worrying and believing it must solve all things by itself, for it sees itself as alone.

All the while I am here, forever pouring forth my goodness, insight, wisdom, peace, love, harmony and joy upon your life. I am forever available to share my glad tidings with you, and to show you the True Reality of all things. I am here to bring healing and transformation to the parts of self that live out of fear and unhappiness, to show you how the limited version of reality is untrue and unjustified in the divine sense of things.

There is a whole new way to live and be, to live as an unburdened child knowing freedom and peace. Holding to my presence and releasing yourself of beliefs that have kept you bound to an unhappy set of ever-revolving circumstances, I come to bring you fully into joy, the Joy of my Divine Presence, which is real, true, and eternal, and which is always available to you each moment of each day.

I live in the Eternal Realm knowing only goodness, happiness, joy, and peace. I watch as you wade through the earthly life beset by problems and fears. Ever I would gladly relieve you of the traumas and turmoil, showing you an easier way if you would but turn to me each moment and hand your life, your troubles, and your problems over to me.

For I heal all conditions. I dissolve all unrealities. I consume all illusions that truth may prevail, so that which is real, true, and eternal may be your constant guide, your continual experience, your fulfillment of your earthly walk as you claim your freedom in the Light Eternal.

I am ever with you, holding the Divine Perfection, which is the Divine Blueprint for your Soul. I hear a planet in travail and I seek to free you from its grip that the Dark Night may pass over and leave you untouched. This is my will for you.

Claim it for yourself. Embrace it with all that you are and know it is my Eternal Gift of goodness that awaits you every moment, which I am pouring out to you so that you may turn to me and receive all that I have prepared for you, all that I am gifting you, all that I am willing for you for yourself. I am the Inner Creative Self.

# Ancient Song of the Soul

*At last a glimpse of Eternity shines through the Dark Night.*
*That which is real and Eternal has stayed.*
*That which was a manifestation of the Unreal Self has been dissolved.*
*Now you begin to live life in True Freedom.*

*-Babaji*

O, Illustrious One, your glimmering light shines forth to awaken, transform, heal, uplift, and inspire all. We, your vessels, the Inner Creative Selves of the souls of humanity, radiate your presence through us to all humankind.

Beloved One, we are a Vessel of Divine Love, a love that is compassionate, considerate, and kind. In all ways we radiate the Presence of Love where we are, and many souls are fed and nourished by our Light. We enter dark times undaunted, for we know we dwell in eternity and therefore, the same laws of life apply to us as the Heavens for we are heaven born.

Therefore, we release the Ancient Song of the Soul, the Ancient Lyrics that are the Sacred Songs*. We are the vessel of these songs to a world entering the Great Travail. In that time, when all souls are called to a reckoning of their karma and are to face their miscreations, the Sacred Songs will ring through their homes reminding them of the Homeland, of that which dwells in Eternity and is true.

As the unreality is stripped away and the nightmare of created realities is upon them, they will find comfort, solace, and respite as the Sacred Songs sing to their souls, soothe their souls and bring them the Light Eternal midst the Dark Night.

Beloved One, as you have kept so close to me anchoring my Light where you are, I am able to position you where you can be of the greatest service and receive the greatest growth during the times ahead. Now I am in full control of your reality and world. Now I can bring my perfection where you are, even in the midst of a Dark Night on Earth and the shuddering of worlds, as many pass through the Great Travail.

I choose to move you out of this reality and to remind you of your true homeland in the heavens. I bring you to a place of safety for a time of resting and restoring, of renewal and healing, err you move out into the world again in service. A place of peace where you can continue to live the Temple Life that I have created for you and to dwell in Eternal Realities with me knowing that first and foremost in your life.

You will see many things in this life, experience many realities, and journey to many lands. It is a long life, full and blessed. For now, trust me as I move you to a consciousness that will give you solace and peace for a time, which will assist you to further unplug from society and its mechanisms, finding your true powers in my presence with you, mastering these qualities rather than attempting to find success in the outer world. Your True Success lies in mastery and attainment, in enlightenment and the restoration of your body temple that it may be divine.

A simple temple life lived in elegant simplicity. A beautiful reality that longs for your arrival, for then you shall have a glorious destiny with wonderful people who long to share their hearts and souls with you and be inspired by your many gifts of Sacred Song. A time of wondrousness in the midst of the darkest night on Earth, can you imagine that?

Beloved One, I prepare many things for you that you will shortly come to comprehend, for you do not know the special powers I have in making all things right for you. You have not known how astute I am on world affairs and how I have guided you to the perfect places at the perfect moments. Never fear, for you have lived among the Nephilim in times past and though the world may come under complete Nephilim rule, you can survive living in purity and simplicity, not buying into their reality nor choosing to live in the midst of their drama. There are many safe havens on Earth and I can take you swiftly to one.

Now you know how precious you are to me and how much I care for you. As you hold your consciousness with me, know that I am ever moving you out of harm into safety. Thus all our momentous work is about clearing you of every last vestige of dark momentums that would keep you entangled or entrapped in the earthly drama.

In the times ahead, you will know of what I speak and be heartened by my foresight, acknowledging how you were moved out of danger at the eleventh hour and how it shall always be so. I will always work with you to keep you safe from harm. For my intention is ever for the highest good for you, peace, tranquility, and ease, grace, blessedness, and wondrousness, enjoying the Magic of Life.

Know that I am ever with you. Continue TheQuest work and you will see how swiftly you become free of the karma now descending upon the world for recompense.

I love you and bless you, my Beloved, my Treasured One. Know the gifts of many great events that will swiftly take you to a whole New Life. In Peace, Serenity, and Ease, I Am your Inner Creative Self.

*The Sacred Songs referred to are songs sung in a Universal Language of Love, that were released directly from the Heavens through Aurora in 1997 and 1998. They are on the albums she co-produced with renowned multi-instrumentalist, Bruce BecVar: *River of Gold, Renaissance of Grace* (Aurora's solo album), and *Gypsy Soul: Heart of Passion.* More about the Sacred Songs in the appendix. To purchase Aurora's Healing Music for an Awakening World, go to http://aurorajulianaariel.com/products/music, and/or http://www.AEOS.ws.

# The Grand Experiment

*All the stalwart souls who revere the Light Within,*
*will reach that attainment whereby they claim*
*their Divinity in this life.*
*Each focused intention carries them*
*across the sea to their True Self.*

*-Babaji*

O, Glorious Day! O, Heaven's Wonders! How graciously you have cast your Light upon this world and filled it with your Supreme Love. How blessed are we to drink in the Sweet Nectar of your Divine Bliss, to see you in all things and to embrace the glory of each precious day.

My Beloved, the Sweet Nectar of Divine Bliss is the Essence of Christhood, the Essence of your Divinity. For entering the bliss and drinking of its nectar, one finds themselves completely enraptured with the Divine Life. There is no other comparison for all falls short of the beauty, magnificence, and truth that dwell in Spirit.

Often I have spoken of the Glorious Realms where only Truth, Beauty, Harmony, and Love is known. I have shared the wonders of a life lived solely true to the highest ideals. To drink in the Everlasting Peace which is your Divine Birthright is to enter the Gates of Freedom and to know you have arrived at the other side, that you have gained access into Realms of Light and not only as a visitor, but as a resident.

I speak to you of this life to remind you that Earth and its conditions are but swirling realities revolving around center cores of illusions, and these can never know the beauty and magnificence of the Heaven Realms from whence you have come, from whence you were born, and to where you will return when you have won your Eternal Freedom.

All that happens here on Earth is but a shadow of the true realities. It is but a mirrored attempt to embrace Heaven's ideals. And yet, with the entanglement of mankind's energies, miscreations that have gone on for so long now, there is only a semblance at times of the Glory of Heaven, only a whisper, a shadow of what lies beyond the Great Sea of miscreated substance.

I draw you now into my being, casting away the shadows and the memories of past days when shadow ruled your life. I draw you up swiftly into my Heavenly Embrace so that you can drink of the Sweet Nectar of Divine Bliss and know True Freedom.

I long for you to cast off every shadow and to choose Heaven for your life experience, wholly and absolutely, claiming it as your own, nevermore to return to shadowed lands and shadowed realities. All this can be done while you remain on Earth. That is the Divine Mystery. That is the great opportunity that stands before you. In the midst of a world in turmoil, you can claim your Eternal Victory and anchor that as a physical reality in this world.

Can you make that everlasting link to Spirit and stay connected while the world enters its greatest travail? Having claimed the true reality, the True Life, can that sparkle across the world, its sweet essence touching many souls and lifting them as well into the Divine Life?

That is the Grand Experiment launched from the Heaven Realms, and why you were all born into the Earth at this crucial time. As you look around, you will see many asleep and they may sleep through the Great Travail, not knowing how to claim their Eternal Victory in the Light. Then, there are the Dark Ones, who utilizing mankind's misuses and past karma, weave a web of spells around the unsuspecting ones in an attempt to enslave a world, but will they succeed?

That is the missing equation, because there is a world filled with Awakening Ones, shining hearts and shining souls who would do more, who would rise on Wings of Freedom and claim their Divine Reality, and this is our hope, the great hope in the Heavens, that Light will overcome darkness, and that darkness will be swallowed up by the Great Light.

TheQuest work is key for this. When you do it, healing takes place within the systems of Earth anchoring the Light and the True Reality where the Darkness was, transforming and healing the darkness, changing it back into the Light of God that never fails.

You and many others work at this time to anchor Light, Truth, Freedom, Hope, and Peace on Earth. Through Love, this light is spreading, enveloping, and embracing humanity. As the Dark Night rolls in, many astute souls rise to meet it, to heal it, and to heal themselves, understanding the outer Shadow is but a reflection, a mirror to the Inner Shadowed Self that must be healed, must be transformed err the victory is won.

Thus the missing equation is the Great Healing that is taking place causing the Great Awakening, as many souls turn to the Light of their God Presence and seek Peace, Truth, Harmony, and Love. As they seek, they shall find the Everlasting Freedom their hearts and souls long for, and this may turn the Dark Night into the Glorious Day.

In the midst of the Great Travail many souls will win their Eternal Freedom. You, my Beloved, are positioned exactly for that victory this day. Keep on and know the glory of these times and that you, with the Ascended Hosts and Elohim, have a very special part to play. Know that it is a Grand Experiment, one in which you agreed to participate because your love for Earth was so great and your longing for Ultimate Freedom was so grand, it propelled you to be here at this time.

Suffer not, nor hide your head in dismay, but face the Night and heal it with your mighty skills. Heal everything you see from within and let TheQuest rule your days each step of the way.

I bring you to the Safe Abode, the Sanctuary of Light, where you can assist humanity from the Place Prepared. Living the Temple Life, you can hold the balance for a world in travail and keep the vigil of healing and transformation at this crucial time.

In love and peace, I hold you eternally in the Light. I am the Inner Creative Self.

# The Life Victorious

*Transcendent experiences*
*teach the Soul that it is Divine.*

-Babaji

Beloved One, Great is the portent of this day as you step fully into our Shared Destiny. Light filled expressions of Divine Love pour from the Heavens. This is the time long awaited. The time long prepared and at last, it has arrived and you are stepping into your New Life.

This Life is nothing like what you have lived before because the human self is now out of the equation. As each day you seek to heal and transform the patterns of the past and hold steadily to the Light which I Am, a wondrous light pours forth through you touching many. It is the Life Victorious, the life most glorious where each breath of each day is precious.

I am with you so fully now, Beloved. You cannot know my joy as you have come away from the world and all its seeming glories to dwell eternally with me. To seek me first above a clamoring world is to know I can gift you every treasure you would ever desire, for I see all and know your heart's greatest ideals, and these I bring to you richly and fully in your present life experience.

We are in the conclusion of many years of your striving for ideals only I could hold for you. In seeking these in the outer world, you came across many barriers, challenges, and difficult life situations and much sorrow. Suffering was your experience. Now I teach you the simplicity of living in joy and this will continue as you completely free your self from the world, its momentums and the momentums of the Shadowed Self.

Dearest One, I sing Hosannas in the highest as our work together has begun. The beautiful simplicity of Sacred Living is now enfolding you in a way of life where you will be prepared at every moment to be available for a mighty outpouring of light from the Heavens. You will be a vessel of my Divine Love in the world, which is the most radiant quality you embody with such effortlessness and sincerity.

You are a great lover of the world in a mother's sense for you would wrap your arms around this world, sing away its troubles in a sacred lullaby, and watch the Dark Night flee from your Loving Presence. Safe in your arms, you would guard the world from any more evils, watching over it that it might know tranquility, ease, and peace. This is our work together as we uplift humanity to its true identity and raise the world into its rightful place in the heavens.

It is a glorious work and yet, more exciting and simple than you could have ever imagined. This will become more evident through these precious times ahead where you live in loving splendor, drinking in the beauty, magic, and love that I have prepared for you.

Gifting you is the greatest joy of my life. Giving you everything you have longed for, held for, idealized, and held sacred in your heart is the greatest destiny for me. Know this absolutely and look to me for all things. For I am your joy, your completeness, your oneness, your hope, the bastion of freedom and treasure house of all you hold precious and dear.

Faster and faster the energies will swirl around you, transforming your life into the Eternal Reality that awaits you but steps away. Keep on and know I am with you, watching over you and gifting you with all that you will ever need to win your Eternal Victory. I am the Inner Creative Self.

# Ascended Master Sponsorship

*Glorious, Victorious, Transcendent and*
*Wondrous is your Life ahead.*

*-Babaji*

My Beloved One, Precious Angel of my Heart, the Light of Peace be with you as I fill you with all my transcendent wonders, multitude of God Qualities and array of Divine Aspirations.

The light on your pathway is great this day for many Ascended Masters have come to sponsor, assist, and to rally with you as you set clear intentions around your finances, endeavors, destiny, and relationships. Because of your clarity of intent and purpose and willingness to undergo whatever healing and transformation is called upon to clear past patterns and limitations, you now have beloved Ascended Masters sponsoring your life.

These ones have arrived to accelerate your path and to bring your endeavors under God Dominion and Control that you, your relationships, your endeavors, your destiny and livelihood may be used to benefit the planet during this time. Therefore, the aspirations of a lifetime inspired on high through your communion with me are now realized as you make your last trek to the homeland through the completion of your earthly cycles.

In joining your efforts with others for a greater purpose, and with intention, vowing to clean up your finances and every area of your lives out of alignment with the Divine Intention, you make yourselves worthy vessels for the Great Light that shall be pouring through you.

Much promise lies ahead through the unity you will now experience with the blessed Ascended Masters who have come to work with you on behalf of humanity. They shall now overshadow your finances, like Great Benefactors watching over your assets, bringing you to a place of safety where you will be free to create more and more blessings for humanity in alignment with my Divine Intention for you. Thus, great things abound and great portents have arisen for you. Hold fast to the light and know I am ever with you. I am the Inner Creative Self.

LETTER TWENTY ONE

# Divine Promise
# of Our Union

*Treasures in Heaven are incomparable
to what one finds on Earth.
But one taste of the Divine Nectar, Bliss,
and one is cured, never to seek Earthly treasures again.*

*-Babaji*

Angel of My Heart, today I live in the Radiant Joy of our promise, the Divine Promise of our Union, because you are so diligent and
I am ever willing your complete and absolute freedom. Beloved, you
cannot know how many people your work reaches nor to what extent
you are assisting a vast change in planetary affairs and consciousness.
In diligently untying all the entanglements from your own life, you are
helping to unweave the causes and cores of hardship, struggle, and suffering on Earth.

Each day, a great work is accomplished as the suffering ones are
healed and the Earth freed from one more facet of unreality. Many are
being released at deep inner levels because you live and will the Earth
to be free.

I move you ever closer to safety and security in a whole new consciousness you have never seen before. A Place Prepared, where you can
live in freedom and truth and raise yourself into the Final Victory, even
as you continue your Sacred Alchemy on behalf of the planet.

There is much work to do err this world is clear of its strangling
unreality, and many will choose suffering as a way to free themselves
and find their own truth in a tumultuous world. Meanwhile, I will hold
you in my arms of safety and protect you from all harm. I will assist you
to live true to your highest ideals, basking in the warm sunlight, playing

in the crystal warm sea, singing beautiful sacred songs, and finding true love in complete harmony and oneness with the Inner Beloved.

Let me show you the way to live in absolute harmony with the Earth. Let me show you how to revel in the goodness and beauty that is everywhere around you, even if others choose a harder way, a more arduous trek. Still you can unplug from this society. You can free yourself from every entanglement and know peace.

You can strive for your perfection and wholeness and with each day, affect the Earth profoundly, beautifully, and majestically with your Inner Work. All this from a beautiful place prepared, where Beauty reigns supreme and where happiness and lightheartedness fill your days.

So much goodness awaits you, my Beloved. Many changes happen now. Swiftly they come, for through your Inner Work you have altered your commitment to life. Now, you can serve away from the turmoil, not engaging in the Great Travail. You can live in your own reality, true to Divine Ideals, which keep you ever alive and free.

I shall teach you many things when your days become still and silent. Silent in the Heaven Realities, in the sacred moments as you walk the vast empty beaches and mountains, communing with me and knowing our union more completely. This I long for.

I am grateful you have come to this place of safety within, that I may provide a safe vantage point with which to radiate my Presence, Love and Light through you. Now is the time to enter the Greater Mystery... the Place of Peace within, and frolicking in the Garden of Eden with me, learn of ever-new joys.

Be at peace and continue the Inner Work, for each day you change the probabilities bringing yourself into freedom and joy. I salute you with much Gratitude. I am the Inner Creative Self.

# The Sacred Garden

*Dance with the Joy of Spirit, the Joy of Reunion with the One,*
*for that is the True Life you seek.*

-Babaji

The Journey of the Heart brings you to the Sacred Garden, the blessed Place of Peace within that lies far from the outside world, its turmoil, longings, and experiences. In this garden is the True Self, the true Beloved of your Heart, the one who holds all the freedom, security, happiness, and peace, the one that knows only perfection and never leaves its happy abode no matter what is taking place in the outer world.

It is time for you to forsake the world that has for so long kept you entrapped and enthralled with all its exciting happenings. The flurry of activities and the dramas within the lives of everyone you know have kept your attention fixed on the outer life, the outer reality, and away from the stillness and peace of the True Self.

The Sacred Garden is as wondrous as any earthly garden, with beautiful flowers and fragrances that are Divine Healing Essences. Within it's grounds there is a glory, a perfection and a peace not known in the earthly realms. It is this peace everyone seeks and this perfection all strive for many times unknowingly.

Being raised on ideals that put financial and physical successes before the Divine Success that would crown your life with its fullest glory, the Soul remains entrapped in earthly living, earthly dramas, as the centuries pass. And where is Freedom, Peace, and Truth? Where can they be found? Where can the weary traveler of lifetimes rest her head and find solace, respite, and rest?

In a hectic world there is no peace. In a succession of dramas and experiences to overcome and meet with strength, fortitude, and intelligence, where is the surcease, the calm, tranquil life many know exists and yet, which is never found on Earth even in the remotest villages?

The Peace of your Life is within you. It resides in the Sacred Garden where the True Self dwells. It is where beauty meets Divine Perfection and where all blessings of healing, grace, and good fortune flow forth.

It has been said, seeking the Kingdom of Heaven first, all else will be restored unto you and that is truth. For the God Presence holds all the wisdom, truth, intelligence, prosperity, and wealth you could ever seek. When it is bestowed, it is bestowed with purity and grace. It is not fraught with problems and conditions. It is freely given and purely received. It is a Divine Essence and it knows no change, no transitory fleetingness like earthly endeavors, earthly successes, and earthly encounters.

The Peace of your Life is within. It is the inner knowing and inner trust of the Divine. Making that relationship personal, it is the bonding or union with the I Am, the True Self. In this union, the Garden of Delight, the Sacred Garden of divine realities and divine qualities opens up and pours its blessings upon you.

Learn to wait upon the direction of the Divine One within. Learn to follow the Inner Wisdom it would share with you. Learn to wait for confirmations in life directions from within rather than running here and there because experiences and projects look exciting or fulfilling. Learn to hold out for what is really true for you. Be true to self in all ways, true to the Divine Self. Learn to listen carefully each day, making yourself available to Spirit through silent meditation and inner communion.

It is then you will feel centered and empowered from within and will become a bastion of light and hope for a world in transition. Anchoring with the God Self in Qualities Divine, your light is spread throughout the world as its essence is released upon the ethers.

So much great good can come from Enlightened Ones who walk upon this Earth completely centered and anchored in the Divine Presence. So much can be transferred through the blessings of an Awakened One, for the airwaves carry essences, Divine Essences that uplift, inspire, awaken, and bless a world from within. They are like flower essences that have healing qualities. How much more powerful is the essences that are wholly Divine?

This is a worthy endeavor, to become enlightened and thereby share your True Essence with the world. There is no other path as noble, as victorious, as astounding, nor exciting. There is no other endeavor as fulfilling and rewarding as finding your Self in the Sacred Garden, becoming the Truth of who you are. There is no other act as momentous as releasing the Shadowed Self back into the flame as a miscreation who over time grew and became the personality, the personal self who believed it was a separate entity from God and yet, all the while sustained and drew its life from the God Presence within.

Blinded by its own self indulgence and ignorance, it has lived on, parading itself as a giant among humankind, all the while building up a life based on unrealities and meaningless endeavors, thinking in some way these things would feed it, nourish it, and give it peace. Thinking if only it had more money, wealth, friends, power, or prestige, it would be happy, successful, and fulfilled.

Countless human lives given over to this focus have found after much energy, striving, and sacrifice, it was all emptiness in the end. An empty shell with no great meaning for these conditions so sought after were devoid of the Divine Essence, the Divine Spirit that would have infused the Soul with all the fulfillment, joy, and peace it could ever desire.

Life is so much more simple then this and yet, the Super Achievers believe their glory lies in outer attainment and thus, their whole expression is given to the outer life of accumulating and getting for an end, for wealth, power, or prestige.

Even great achievements of a humanitarian nature many times are enacted and brought forth out of the need to be important, to feel good about oneself, to feel secure. All the underlying patterns that keep the soul driven also keep the Soul from discovering what is really of value in it's life, what would give it the deepest meaning, what would bring the greatest happiness and fulfillment.

I am here today to share with you the Secret Alchemy of turning within, of claiming the Divine Life and of building one's life momentum upon the Divine Union with the True Self and nothing other. Putting this awakening first and foremost and letting everything else in one's life come under God Dominion and God Control. This is the Path to Happiness, the way to move from the sorrowful, unfulfilled life into the exciting, spontaneous, spectacular life of the Divine Self.

Claim your divinity each day, Beloved. Seek that divinity even while you wrestle with patterns of the past that would choke you and give you a lesser experience. Take a step away from the world in seeking this Life Divine and allow me to bring you to the place of safety and peace, which is an inner condition that can then be mirrored by a more perfect outer reality than you could have ever created on your own.

Cease seeking successes in the outer world and go for the one true success of being fully enlightened and free in this life. It is the way I have been calling you to for lifetimes. In this lifetime, you can claim it for sure. I am the Inner Creative Self.

# Promise of the Ages

*Light is at the end of the tunnel*
*as you traverse the vast regions of the Self*
*to discover who you really are.*

-Babaji

Radiant and wondrous is this day, a day created with much glory, enlightenment, and peace. We who dwell in the Heaven Realms, look down upon Earth with hearts filled with love overflowing. For humanity is being redeemed from the deepest darkest caverns of the Shadowed Self to the heartfelt yearnings of sincere and devoted hearts. This day freedom is ringing forth.

This is a freedom of the soul with infinite possibility in the realm of the Infinite One where darkness gives way to light, the Dark Night to day, and the sleeping unawareness of the soul to the Awakening of the Spirit.

All who seek and yearn for this freedom will find it. All who set their course to see this freedom fulfilled will win it. All those who are one pointed in their devotion to the Light will know the Awakening of their True Selves midst the darkness of the Shadowed One. Out of darkness will be born a New Light, as out of a darkened Earth will be born a New Song.

This is my promise, the Promise of the Ages. Light overcomes darkness, because darkness is only an appearance, an overlay of energy upon the vast Presence of God. Therefore, what was created with God's energy can be recreated instantly, transformed back into its true essence, the Eternal Light.

For a time, the light within was clothed in unreality. So, can the soul come back into its True Estate and know the freedom of its inherent longing. Darkness can be turned back into its true essence, the Light, just as the Shadowed Self can be turned back into its True

Essence, the Divine Self. All this can take place with TheQuest work, which facilitates an Inner Transformation of Self.

Dearest One, all appearances in this world no matter how dire can be healed. Every last condition can be transformed, first in the deepest core of its manifestation, the unconscious beliefs of humanity and the outplaying of the pictures it has held.

Understand, the Innate Creative Life Force is continually creating and bringing forth after the images of humankind, which are the unconscious beliefs, patterns, vows, wills and intentions. All these images can be healed and transformed swiftly and absolutely, never more to plunder, cause detriment, nor destroy the great focuses of the Earth.

This Earth was created in innocence, purity, and a perfect God Design. It was gifted to a humanity who over time decided they needed to have a lesser more painful experience than the glory of the Garden of Eden. Many turned away from the perfection and began to believe in imperfection, darkness, hardship, toil, and all other conditions that are now taken for granted today as a normal way of life.

In truth, these are all miscreations, mishaps that can be changed back into the Eternal Reality of Oneness and Truth, Beauty and Perfection, Majesty and Grace, Love, Harmony, and Peace.

All God Qualities that would pour their essence upon this world are held back because humankind has instated miscreations in their place. The Divine Perfection that would easily prevail on Earth, gifting all and healing every last condition, must await a humanity who has willed a different reality, a reality filled with wars, fighting, turmoil, unhappiness, grief, crimes, destruction, and all that is an antithesis to the Divine Estate.

Know and understand, all these things that have been created on Earth can be swept away, can be consumed by Elohim, dissolved by the Holy Light of God. Perfection, Peace, Harmony, and Joy can reign on Earth again, can be invited through open pure hearts to visit. When humanity makes room for Heaven, it can stay on Earth forevermore.

Believe in the ancient histories that speak of past glorious ages, Golden Ages where humankind lived in perfection and truth and where all that you see today did not have its presence in the world. For the world dwelled in purity, wholeness, and oneness, and all things reflected the Divine Essence, this Divine Perfection.

Have faith in that which is unseen. Have faith in the One who works a Sacred Alchemy through you. Have faith in the Legions of Light that work continually on behalf of humanity healing, restoring, and repairing the fabric of the Earth. Have faith and know that in your lifetime you will see many things, many wondrous events taking place all in Divine Perfection.

For a time, I sweep you away from humanity to a Sacred Abode where you will be free to fully awaken and know me as I truly am, which is your self. Know as I prepare this place within you, I live in joy and knowledge of all that will be shortly fulfilled, the promise of our ever-growing union, our oneness that is the most precious gift in the universe for me.

I bring you apart from the world that you will know yourself in your absolute Divine Reality and from this vantage point I teach you many things. In your Sacred Place prepared, we gift the world in unique ways, in the world but not of it, living at a time of Great Travail, but not participating in it. Living in Truth and Joy in the midst of the last appearances of hell before it is completely swallowed up and vanquished.

This day is glorious for it denotes one more step towards our complete union. Thus the birds sing the sweet melodies of our oneness and nature performs its glorious work in uplifting and inspiring your heart heavenwards. Blessings abound and all is peace, happiness, and joy.

Live in Heaven with me today and continue to step into the glorious future with me where I dwell in perfection in your world. I am the Glorious One, the herald of glad tidings of wondrous joy and peace. I am the Infinite One, dwelling within you, yet living fully in the Heavens. Solve that mystery and know me as I am. I am the Inner Creative Self, the Blessed Divine Presence within you.

# Sacred Alchemy

*Regions of the psyche must give way to the Light of the I Am.*
*Only then, can the Wondrous Presence pour her Truth*
*into your consciousness, being, and world.*
*It is then that Heaven on Earth is born in your life experience.*

*-Babaji*

Blessings abound, Beloved, as you reap the rich rewards of harmony, truth, and grace, pouring the vast wealth of ancient mysteries, knowledge, and truth into your Soul Expression. Vast fields of knowledge and accomplishments are now being accessed on the deepest levels of being as you open fully to my truth, to my Light and to our oneness.

So much is being released to you. If you have found yourself sleeping longer and more deeply, it is because you are undergoing many great internal shifts, and these shifts in consciousness are now reverberating throughout your whole consciousness, being, and world, affecting every level of your being.

These are wondrous times as you come to blend with my light more fully. Drinking of the Sweet Elixir of your Divinity, you come to know yourself fully as Divine. All you have traversed that was an outcome of a lesser nature, a lesser consciousness, is now being dissolved by the Mighty Light which I Am, is now being consumed from even the memory banks that have held all the records of iniquities and failings.

Opening your life to my presence is clearing out the old records and replacing all with the Divine Qualities and Divine Intention for your life. This is wiping clean records of iniquities that have bound the Soul and kept it recreating after false patterns. In removing these deep within the psyche, the Soul is free to create after the Divine Image.

Whatever the patterns are, whether human or Divine, that is what will be amplified and magnified in the Soul's experience. Therefore, the ever creative principle which I am, is continually magnifying the patterns and bringing them into fruition. It is necessary to clear all patterns that are imperfect and limiting to the Soul Expression if you would create the perfection of the Heaven Realms on Earth.

Recreating Heaven is as easy to me as it is to the Elohim, vast powerful creative beings as they are. For it is exchanging energy fields, transmuting them and raising them into a higher vibration or frequency. As this is done, the outcome is altered. Where there would be strife in the Soul's future, now will be harmony, where there would be falsehoods, now will be Truth. Where there were failings and iniquities will be purity, wholeness, and rightness.

It is very simple to transform the patterns through the Inner Work you have called TheQuest. It is a powerful Sacred Alchemy that alters reality, past, present, and future and yet, it never alters the everpresent Divine Essence, which is your innate energy pattern and field from which you have created new images over or upon it.

If you do not like what you have created and the outcome that has resulted, you can change it by healing and transforming the patterns, returning the energy field that held these patterns back into the Divine Essence.

Then, all outcomes will be of a Divine Nature or Divine Intention rather than a human mess up. For the human way is limiting. It is from a Shadowed Self rather than a Divine Self. Therefore, the creations will always be less than the perfection one finds in the Heaven Realms, where all things are created perfectly from the divine patterns and images.

Now you have the Sacred Alchemy Secret behind TheQuest work and how very simple it is. Some conditions seem locked in and therefore take an effort to recreate, especially if they have become physical. The mental and emotional planes are far easier and faster to clear, but the physical realities can be altered and far more quickly then one thinks by diligent effort.

In healing and transforming life conditions, one becomes unbound by karmic recompense and instead comes under Divine Laws and the Divine Way of Life. This is an altered state than what is mostly lived on Earth today, but it can be anchored into the physical realm when the energy field of the patterns have been cleared and transformed back to Divine Patterns. Simply said, one can recreate their life experience choosing the Divine Way instead of the human way of limitation and struggle. This is what is meant by returning to Eden and by drinking of the Elixir of the Divine Essence.

Living in Truth, Beauty, and Divine Perfection is a Way of Life for countless souls who have made the trek to freedom before you. These live in Heaven Spheres that know only perfection and peace. Far from the turmoil of Earth's Travail, these ones live in absolute harmony with the Divine, their true heritage and inheritance won.

How many spheres of perfection reign in this galaxy would be an astounding amount to your mind, for you have adapted so much to Earth thinking and Earth time. You can barely conceive of other spheres of perfection, having reaped so much imperfection here. Yet it is true. There are wondrous spheres that do not know hardship, struggle, disease, toil, or death. For these qualities are of a human nature, not Divine.

They were humanly created, changing Eternal Life for temporal life and holding this as a temporary Earth Pattern that all have accepted as a Way of Life. And yet, there are even some on Earth who know their Eternal Freedom. They do not frequent current Earth societies often. Rather, they stay in their Illumined State working with those that are rising from the dark mire of the nightmare of Earth, those who are seeking rarer fields of consciousness and cosmic truths that have been forgotten and ignored here.

A society built upon Temporal Power and temporal realities must eventually be undone, for it has not built and created out of the Divine Image, which is Eternal. As consciousness is, so shall the manifestation be, and the outcome prevail.

Until this is changed within, you will never see physical realities come close to the Divine Realities known in many spheres. Freedom will remain a dream of the Soul rather than a physical, tangible, reality.

Keep on the great work of transforming every life condition and pattern and see how easily, gently, and swiftly your life will continue to change into the Divine Reality. I Am the Inner Creative Self.

# Abundance and Wealth Your Divine Birthright

*Peace, Tranquility, and Ease are
the prerequisites of the Enlightened Soul.*

-Babaji

Prosperity flows forth in an abundant array. Wealth streams in and fills your life completely. All lack diminishes and is never known again in any form. The last steps of financial dis-ease gives way to a glorious New Life of Prosperity and Peace, of tranquil moments basking in the Abundance and Wealth I have prepared for you. For I will it so, and so shall it be.

At last a surcease, an end to the turmoil, lack, difficulty, strain, and all its stressfulness, all the wearing and tearing it has done, undermining your faith in Divine Providence and that I am here to provide everything for you.

Your life has been so full of this turmoil, this strain and yet, every step through it you have remained the Faithful One. Faithful and true to the Cause, aligned with Divine Purpose and willing to give your all for a humanity on the verge of Enlightenment and Peace, because you have chosen to dream this vision into reality. You have lived the life of a saint and I acknowledge these qualities in you. You have chosen to release yourself from the patterns of martyrdom that no longer serve and which have kept you in financial lack so continually.

Now the last of the financial unrest is removed. Like a huge dark cloud, it is swept out of your reality never to return. Great work has been done on deep inner levels through your clear intentions and devotion to my will. Therefore, I have willed your freedom on every level and most especially this day, your Financial Freedom. So be it.

I have had enough of your struggle, lack, strain, and stress while holding such noble ideas and ideals, desiring to gift your children the very best in life, and committed to humanity's advancement. Therefore, I decree this day you are free financially. I now bring into your world a steady stream of wealth, prosperity, ease, tranquility, and knowledge of my ever-present Grace.

For I am with you, Beloved, overseeing every aspect of your life. As you have committed your life energies to me, surrendering every last desire, hope, and dream that my will may reign supreme, so do I gift you with my Eternal Love in physical, tangible form, bringing contentment and ease, safety and trust in my Beneficent Will for you.

I love you and I will not stand for one more erg of financial distress in your world. Even as you would give your all to remove the strain and struggle from your children's lives, so I am there for you. In the days to come you will know this absolutely in a physical way for I have willed it so. I will that you know you can trust me completely to change every last condition of stress, illness, and dis-ease into the Divine Harmony, Prosperity, and Oneness that was intended. You can trust and put your absolute faith in me and reap tangible rewards in physical realities that will alter your life forever

I will it so, therefore it is done. Watch my power descend in a mighty flash of Light. Watch my will, like lightening, cast away the Dark Night and bring in the New Day. Watch my alignment of absolute Financial Freedom manifest swiftly in your physical reality sweeping away, once and for all, financial lack of every kind.

I will and so it is done and forever shall be. As you hold with me and claim my will for you, so will the miracles descend. I know your heart. I know your ideals. I know the dreams that lie in your heart of hearts. Therefore, you can trust me to fulfill all you hope and dream and desire without the need for you to go out and seek this in the world. For my will is supreme. Aligning with my will, everything can manifest physically immediately, bringing every last dream and vision alive before you in perfect form, even more perfect than you have imagined it.

I am here to raise your belief in me once and for all, to show you that you can place your whole trust in me. I choose to show you through healing your finances, instating wealth in its place. Therefore, be prepared for a great descent of prosperity and financial well-being immediately in your world. When it descends, understand this is but one area I would bless your life. Hold with me then. We together will manifest all of your dreams. This vision will pour forth its beneficent Wisdom, Prosperity and Light upon a world that longs for your essence.

Beloved, be of good cheer, for the tidings I bring tonight will manifest physically before you can believe it would come true, for I am absolute and immediate. I am aligned with all the Highest Intentions for you. I hold you in the absolute light of Transcendent Perfection, your true created state, and long for you to embrace yourself completely in this light.

The Financial Freedom and ease will help. It will take a great weight off your shoulders you have not known you have born and will set you free in many ways. Free to be everywhere I will you to be, whenever I will it. Free to travel to the most exotic places, to gift the world with your message of World Peace, to pour forth the Light of the Heavens to an awakening humanity and now it all begins.

You are the Treasure of my Heart and I love you. I am the Inner Creative Self.

# Know the Glory of Your Divine Plan Fulfilled

*Rest, restore, revitalize your being and*
*know that as the Great Command goes forth,*
*all things are taken care of.*
*Therefore, Peace, Tranquility, and Ease can fill your every day,*
*as you allow the unfoldment of the Perfect Plan.*

*-Babaji*

Beloved One, so valiant and pure. Now is the time to rally up the forces of your destiny. Now is the descent of a Great Light and a great moment. Know the glory of your Divine Plan fulfilled.

For now is the time of glory, the time of Great Advancement, and of lending heart, head, and hand to the valiant effort of humanity's birth into a New Age, the time for you to enter fully into your highest destiny and purpose, to be in perfect alignment with me, as in joy we enter service to life.

Now you understand the journey and all you passed through to enter this day. You understand why I have pulled you apart from society and friends at times to be in retreat, that you can stay ever near to me focused on the One Presence which I am, giving your full allegiance to me. In that way, you have been prepared inwardly and on every level. Your temple has been accelerated and cleansed for the Great Light to descend, your throat chakra purified.

Now it is time. You enter the last part to the wondrous destiny I have prepared for you, which is truly our alignment and focused energy in this world together as one. For in aligning fully with me, your destiny is born. It soars on Wings of Light, free and untrammeled from the world below that spins at a different vibration.

You have begun to see how friends could not remain friends as you moved up in vibration, for their energy fields could not yet contain the Great Light of the I Am. The less evolved ones have moved away out of your field and though there was great love there on your part, there was not the resonant vibration and purity on their part. Rather, a thicker energy veil, field of illusionary substance, forever keeping them on a track of karmic recompense.

You, my Beloved, have moved out of the karmic patterns that once bound you and are stepping free. Now you understand how karmic substance is meant to be purified and returned to its God Essence, not lived out of in suffering and misery.

You see how vibrant, brilliant, wondrous, and precious is God's Love for you, ever-present and always there to uplift, raise, and heal every last condition in your world. As you have created, you can un-create, transform, and raise the energies back into the Divine Essence, and therefore allow the Divine Plan to flow swiftly but gently into your world experience.

The hour is nigh. Many changes happen swiftly to catapult you into a whole new world and a whole new reality. Life, with its many dramas gives way to reveal the Everlasting Truth in your Divine Awareness and Awakening. In the midst of this awakening is your dharma, your Divine Plan. Glorious and precious, it is born into the world in joy, laughter, and fun.

I am the Glorious One, radiant, alive, fearless, undaunted by world affairs and world happenings, which can never touch the perfection of who I Am. I live in peace, harmony, and tranquility every moment of every day, knowing each moment as precious, blessed, enriching, revitalizing, and restoring. I am constantly drinking in the Divine Energies of replenishment, continually being fed by the Magnificent Beauty all around me.

I am the Precious One, the one God holds as Precious, the treasure of his/her heart. I accept my Divine Inheritance fully. I claim beauty, peace, and wholeness as my Life Expression. I know I am Divine and my divinity is secure, solid, and an unalterable fact no matter what I ever experience or perceive, it is.

I live in beauty. I fill my life with magnificence. I revel in the wonders, magic, and miracles of life. I seek only to be free to experience the Divine Essence which I Am, eternally grateful for the blessings that are constantly bestowed. I let go, releasing my hold on circumstances and worldly affairs, knowing as I hold to the I Am, I am continually being fed, cared for, assisted, supported, and guided through life, and that all things in my world are coming under God Dominion and God Control.

I Am that I Am, forevermore living in the Divine Reality of my oneness, unity, and completeness in the Divine Self. I am free, soaring as an eagle above the worldly consciousness, knowing myself as divine, wholly and absolutely. I live in Freedom, move in Freedom, and have my being in Freedom. I live to glorify the One who I Am. This is a statement of truth that can be repeated and reaffirmed every day. I gift it for your use, to assist you to accelerate your path in a tremendous way.

My Beloved, I share with you my divine perspective, that you may know the levels of perfection in which I dwell, which is your True Estate. Rise with me and join me there in the Place of Purity, Perfection, and Truth, where we will live in harmony, happiness, and joy forevermore. I am the Inner Creative Self.

# Treasures of Heaven

*Treachery, lies, and deceit of
others can no longer touch you. You are free!*

-Babaji

Beloved, Treasures of Heaven are being lowered into your physical reality in an abundant array you have not yet known in this life. As your finances clear, the way is prepared for a New Destiny and a New Life, lived true to Divine Purpose in a place prepared that is a Sanctuary of Light and therefore is called the Sacred Haven... a life lived in purity and truth.

A life dedicated to my Divine Will and Intention must reap its rewards and blessings, which are now abounding in your life. So many swift changes will occur as you give your final allegiance to me and the light of who you are, while vestiges of the Shadowed Self find healing and transformation in my Retreat Temple.

I have called you into a life most sacred, a life in service to the Earth and yet, from a safe vantage point where harmony, tranquility, and ease dwell in silent majesty in an abundant land, a Garden of Eden. To this life I call you.

It is not a life for a slumbering soul to wander in the midst of heavenly beauty and be self-indulged. It is a life that gives of itself to humanity in many precious, grace-filled ways and yet, feels this is play... the Divine Play it was called to, born to, and which it lives for.

Treasures of Heaven now abound in your Life experience and expression. The vast array of wondrous jewels clothe you in the Abundant Life you have long sought, as you knew it warranted the time of your Infinite Freedom in the Light, your time of Awakening to the Truth of who you are.

You have known about the Inner Sanctuary of your Soul, for at deep inner levels you have been preparing for this time, a time apart from the world in a Sacred Haven where you could come into complete God Dominion and God Control.

How long have you traversed the earthly wilds encountering many experiences and knowing many expressions, only to find many of these sour compared to the Sweet Nectar of your Divine Reality which I Am.

Now you understand life's equation. Now you see the import of coming into a time of retreat and safety while the world makes its choices whether to live or die. So many choices of the collective unconscious mixed with the Divine Essence and so many different outcomes and probabilities.

You, my Beloved, understand this and work diligently to free yourself of needless outplays of a horrific karma. For you choose to live with me in truth, honesty, purity, and wholeness and thus, a New life is born, a new reality emerges out of the dusk of the Shadowed Self. The Night parts and gives way to the Glorious New Day, which is the dawning of my enthronement on the seat of your being, the true ruler restored. Thus, you are restored and can now turn your attention to Restoration Earth, the project of your heart and your divinity, the cause you were called to Earth to assist in your own precious, unique way.

So many gifts, treasures of my heart, the essence of who I Am and now the Awakening in the opening to Truth as the Night of Unreality is vanquished. The True Life, true career, true wealth, true beloved is now born into your physical reality and anchors completely and absolutely in your world. For it is time for you to gift the world with your precious essence and to live fully and absolutely as a Divine Being in the Earth.

You have your Armor of Light and it shall vanquish the last vestiges of the Night and seal your aura, protect and defend your honor, and seal you from earthly vibrations once harmful. It will keep you relaxed, confident, secure, and restful as the true tranquility I have long wanted to gift you descends and becomes a part of your normal life reality, an everyday occurrence and way of being.

Such joy I share with you, so many victories in such a short time and more and more each day. Now the trumpets sound and your wealth is restored. With it all things are possible. All that I envision, hold for and gift you will now manifest very quickly. Hold to my Divine Matrix, reinforce my Divine Intention, hold for my vision to become manifest in your physical world and all perfection shall be your life experience. It is as simple as that. Hold fast to the Light of the God Presence allowing no other reality, momentum, or desire to enter in, only the intention to be a Vessel of Divine Love and to be aligned with my will for you.

Peace I bring to you this day, peace that will assist you to rest securely, to know you are loved, cared for, assisted, sponsored, and that all perfection is forever manifesting in your life. Your finances restored will give you courage and strength, for you will be free to fulfill everything you have seen, easily and gracefully, without stress or strain.

The days of sorrows, tightness, lack, withholds, hardship, and struggle are gone, vanquished from your kingdom. Now, beauty, loveliness, perfection, harmony, oneness, prosperity, and wealth abound as the New Kingdom arises in the glory of the Golden Age within you. As within, so it is without. Your outer experience now shifts dramatically as it comes into alignment with the Inner Reality, beautifully restored to the Divine Intention.

How joyous I am for this victory to commune with you, the Victorious One. For in allowing my healing and assistance, the way has been made clear for a whole new life to be manifesting for you. Many of the old situations and ways of life have been vanquished, dissolved, and terminated as a life experience. In their place are hundreds of qualities that speak to the Abundant Life you step into... the Glorious Life, the Tranquil Life, the Beautiful Life I have prepared for you.

No matter what the world chooses, you can live in absolute magnificence and wealth from this day forward, for you are no longer connected to the Great Travail. You are a free agent in this world. You are free and becoming freer with each moment, with each clearing, with each healing. True Freedom is in the heart. It is the Fire of Creation unleashed and the perfect creation manifest in your outer world.

Have faith. Understand the portent of these times and know how much I love you, treasure you, and adore you. How deeply I believe in you, have faith in you, acknowledge you, and honor you. How richly I feel your Life Essence, life intention, life destiny. How profoundly I am able to make all things right, clear the way for greater mastery and attainment and bring you into a fully awake state, which is my Divine Intention.

Soon the dream of dreams unfolds as you find yourself living in greater mastery and attainment with an ability to allow a fully functioning Divine Existence as your normal way of life. Then, joy, joy, joy will pour out of every single pore, radiating from your heart and lifting you into ever new merriment, laughter, and fun. Life will teach you, will gift you back your joyous heart, your radiant smile, your happy self and this very soon.

Be at peace, for only joy abounds in your physical reality now, joy, joy, joy in the presence of the One, in the Peace of my Heart. I hold you dear, safe and sound. I champion your honor and fulfill your intention. With an Armor of Light, I enfold you in safety and peace. No more harm shall come to you from any quarter as the causes and cores are healed. In increments, the last foe is vanquished and peace restored within.

Now Peace reigns and good will prevails with Harmony, Light, and Truth in every quarter. Truth shall shatter the darkness and dissolve forever the rumors that have gone out against you, for as you vanquish the Inner Enemy, Inner Gossiper, Inner Maligner, Truth in its most radiant form shall prevail... Peace, Peace, Peace, Peace!

The Sacred Haven awaits you. Soon I shall transport you to this Inner Sanctuary where you will find the gift I am giving you in this Sacred Place Prepared. Then, a most Glorious Life begins with so many blessings, so much richness and truth.

I love and bless you, my dearest one. Have faith, for I speak only truth and you shall know this absolutely and without a shred of doubt once all is fulfilled. In Peace, Harmony, and Love, I am the Inner Creative Self.

# Fill Your Senses With Divine Qualities

*Joy is the Divine Complement to Beauty.*
*Nature resounds with joyful murmuring.*
*Beneath the rush and roar of society is a silent*
*current of Joy wafting upon the senses of humanity,*
*bringing its silent wonder to all who enter the Silence to hear it.*

*-Babaji*

Precious is your heart's intention to commune daily with me, allowing me to pour my magnificence into your world. As you stay attuned to me, I am able to assist you in so many areas of your life, bringing perfection, mastery, and beauty.

There is a simple law and that is, "What your attention is upon, that is where you are and what you focus on you become." Thus, it is simply stated and simply applied that when your attention is on my Divine Perfection and all the blessings I am forever pouring forth upon you, your world opens up to embrace more of my gifts. Taking your attention away from lack, illness, despair, and other earthly qualities, you fill your senses with Divine Attributes.

A glad heart is always well rewarded from those in the Heavens who feel inspired to gift the aspiring one more. Ever open to all the gifts, the wise soul understands this law and makes itself available to receive the plentiful gifts that are continually pouring from the Heavens.

Now you have begun to understand the Grand Equation and to know, "As you believe, so shall it be and what you put your attention on, will you experience and become." It is a matter of connecting with me and then allowing my magnificent qualities, all unique, to shine through you, to radiate simply, easily, and effortlessly out into your consciousness, being, and world.

I am always here with you, available to gift you everything you could ever need and desire and yet, you have not known this. You have not dared to think or dream of the Grand Adventure that comes when you fully align with me and no more imperfection manifests in your world. It is then that True Perfection reigns and the Soul enters the Ascension to live forever free.

If I am always here pouring my perfection into your world, then why are you experiencing lack and upset at times? Why do harsh seasons roll in taking all your effort to keep above the water? Why, when you are so aligned with living true to my will, does imperfection mar your world?

The answer to this is in ages past where accumulations of experiences and beliefs began a very different focus for your soul. Your gaze turned from me as you began thinking new thoughts and expounding on new realities, all of a limiting and harmful nature to you. Instead of the Divine Perfection, which is ever my will and intention, you began to believe that somehow having erred you must suffer, struggle and strife must meet you on life's highways, and you must work hard to sustain yourself in this world. Somehow you have believed you were subject to disease and then to old age and death.

Slowly through the centuries, time moved away from the great and glorious Golden Ages where only perfection was known, into the Dark Ages where humankind's dark thoughts and untoward beliefs became the rule of the day. And thus, suffering, hardship, pain, misery, sorrow, loss, lack, strife, discomfort, torment, torture, and death became known on Earth and dwelled amongst souls that had never known such qualities before.

If my qualities are of a Divine Nature, then what are these qualities that were superimposed upon life, created out of the minds of humanity, who turning away from me, the God Presence within them, embraced and claimed other beliefs and therefore other realities?

It is human willing and wishing evil upon the self and why? What happened to cause such a dissent of consciousness, to cause humankind to embrace qualities foreign to me and to those that dwell in the Heavens, that are foreign to the past Golden Ages and those Heavenly Spheres where perfected beings dwell?

There was a time when the narrow thoughts of humanity brought them to the lowest point ever until they could not fathom my existence, let alone embrace my Divine Attributes. It was a Dark Era and yet, in time, the Light of my Presence pierced the Dark Night of the mind in the collective unconscious of humanity and a New Day dawned. Before that, the descent came suddenly for some, who entered other beliefs and turned to embrace other ways and then, experiencing suffering from those choices, believed they were bad and wrong. With this belief came the belief of punishment and thus, self-enforced punishments became the rule on Earth until now there is so much suffering and so little joy, happiness, and peace.

It is a long history, for humankind has sojourned this planet way before even the records in your history books. There have been many Golden Ages and many Dark Ages, all an experience of the Soul to allow it freedom to create what it will and to learn in its creating, the consequences that come from such a creation.

The great good that comes from this is the personal education gained by each soul through life conditions that cause individuals to understand their responsibility for each creation. In this way, the Soul is groomed for greater and greater responsibility as it turns away from dark creations and chooses to embrace the divine part of itself, manifesting the Divine Qualities that are its True Essence.

Through trial and error, the Soul learns edification. Through the freedom to create as it will with no consequence from the Heavens, only self imposed consequences and self inflicted punishments, it learns about human nature verses Divine Nature and therefore, it finally knows what is of value and what in life is not. That is when the Soul becomes awake and in its awakening, it grows in power and perfection. It learns how to magnify its Divine Potential and how to heal and transform the human equation, which kept it trapped for lifetimes. Then it begins to turn its gaze heavenward and to dream of fairer realities. Magical, mystical moments begin to penetrate the otherwise hard existence and synchronicities become a way of life.

A way opens up never seen before, a simpler, easier way then known or experienced in the past. The bright light of my presence engulfs the mental and emotional bodies and fills them with peace, tranquility, and ease. The way becomes more and more effortless because the Soul understands the game, knows the equation, seeing what brings misery, suffering, and hardship, and what creates happiness, joy, and wellbeing. It is then the Heavens rejoice, because a soul is completing the earthly journey, the long trek through myriad lifetimes, ever growing, ever learning and finally fulfilling its reason for experiencing all it has gone through.

There are arms open wide to greet the Soul, the Valiant One, who entered the Great Darkness and who, in releasing itself of bondage, returned home. There is praise, thanksgiving, and so much love, far beyond what earthlings can imagine. For in that Love, there is no blame, no judgment, and no criticism of what was experienced or encountered. It was a learning, growing experience, giving wisdom and edification to the Soul who wanted to learn what life was like living out of a dark and unknown reality, believing it was separate from me and therefore alone and yet, it was not. There was never a moment we were not connected, that I was not gazing lovingly upon the soul, providing life, breath, and as much as I could gift amidst so many beliefs.

It was only beliefs holding back the Love Tide of Divine Perfection, Abundance, Health, Wealth, Oneness, Harmony, and Truth I forever was releasing to the Soul. Only beliefs it could not have or experience these things kept its awareness focused on different realities it was creating, until at times whole realities of my blessings and gifts were ignored and left unseen, unexperienced, and unacknowledged.

How often the Soul did believe itself alone and suffered in the midst of so much loving and comforting. How many times did it think itself poor and wretched when wealth was my only intention? Forever I have awaited your soul's return so I can gift you, replenish you, revitalize you, and bring your life back into the perfection I intend for you. As you release all beliefs and limitations, you have gathered and determined to have as your life experience, you will witness my gifts constantly pouring into your world and you will wonder how you went about Earth so blind and unknowing.

Life is precious and you, my Beloved, have had quite an arduous, yet fruitful journey. Now I ask that you release and relinquish all those qualities, thought forms, and beliefs that no longer serve you. If they bring unhappiness, then they truly are not my will for you. This is how you can measure whether it is a divine quality or human intention. So simple, so easy, so effortless. I am here forever blessing, uplifting, and raising you into the Light Eternal. Turn your gaze upon me and know me as your Self Divine. I am the Inner Creative Self.

# Radiate My Presence To All You Meet

*Dream the dream of your life into reality.*
*Fearlessly go where no one you know has gone before.*
*Reach out and grasp the Eternal Oneness within your reach.*
*Climb the Mountain of Fulfillment,*
*and let the Essence of your Divine Nature*
*waft upon the airwaves of this world.*

*-Babaji*

Peace, Beloved, the Dark Night draws nigh. This time, it is vanquished by the Eternal Light which I Am. Diligence, fortitude, and confidence is the way to meet it. Through Love it is healed, never to resurface to haunt you again. This is its final hour.

Therefore, be awake. Be aware. Lend your energies to enfold all situations that have cast shadows upon your life with the Light. Embrace the Dark Night as you would a dear friend, for it is the only way to vanquish it forever from your world. Shrink not, nor run away. Rather, stand firmly, boldly, intent upon healing this last vestige of your unconscious that would bring horrific experiences into your world.

You can win the Night and bring in the Day of Everlasting Peace, Beauty, and Harmony that awaits you after this last battle. You can soar like an eagle in flight, nevermore troubled by the murmuring of those on Earth that would do you and your life harm. You can be free, because your internal reality will be free, clear, and in full support of you. Therefore, be not alarmed, but rather know that every opportunity to do this inner healing work will result in your greater freedom and ability to move through this world unharmed.

There are many opportunities for humanity to clear the unconscious realm of deep seated patterns perpetually and actively creating each person's outer reality. Few stop to see the causes and cores, let alone heal them. Therefore, you must understand as you walk through this world, those who are diligently at work to free themselves are few and far between.

Understanding this equation, you keep yourself free from dramas and entanglements by radiating love and light to all. Never engage in challenging belief systems and patterns, as the human nature will revile the one that exposes it. This is a hard lesson and one worthy of understanding, for knowing the way of the world, you can easily avoid hardship and relationship dynamics that would otherwise be painful.

Through the ability to radiate my Presence of Love to all you meet, you are able to dissolve these conditions and the tendency to accuse or criticize, judge or bring attention to another's patterns. Understanding and seeing the patterns is for your own edification. It allows you to make wise decisions concerning people and where to place yourself accordingly.

This information is not to tear them down, bring attention to lower nature aspects, or to disparage, judge, or criticize them, for everyone on Earth has patterns. Yet, few allow the God Presence to radiate forth through their Souls. Therefore, it is rare to find one who walks with the gentleness of the Holy Spirit, radiating love and light to all, remaining detached to earthly natures and earthly momentums.

How is this done when another's patterns are wreaking havoc in your world? How can you continue to radiate love and light when another is abusive? The answer is simple. Go within, for within you lies the cause and core.

Everyone who steps into your field of consciousness is a reflection of an inner condition or aspect of your consciousness. When the individual is radiating their Higher Nature, it is a reflection of your Divine Nature and the beautiful attributes that are also your own inner qualities. When it is of a disturbing nature, it is a call to look deep into the psyche, into the unconscious realm where patterns are being called up to be healed.

The level of upset you feel over a certain circumstance is the level and degree of the intensity in which you must face old patterns. It is a call, a wake up call to be alerted to places within that must be healed and transformed. Invariably, you will find the two inner aspects, many times male and female, acting out their roles in negative unhealthy dynamics that must be healed before you will feel balanced and at peace again.

This healing work is profound, because it leads to Self Discovery, Self Mastery, and Wholeness. The degree you are triggered is the degree in which you must get to work. High intensity means work to be done right now, whereas mild irritation shows a potential for inner work in the future. An accumulation of similar events leads to the uncovering and healing of a major life pattern. Healing and transforming these patterns, you are set free to embody the Presence of Light and Love in the world, to soar in the ecstatic Ocean of Bliss and to revel in the harmony and beauty of Heavenly Delight. All this while on Earth.

I salute your efforts and your diligence. I stand with you to vanquish every Night. First within and then, as is the natural course, the outer reality is transformed. This is Sacred Alchemy, a gift of TheQuest Work. Learn these teachings well, for in this time you are called to relinquish the desire to Expose the Truth and to rather turn within to heal all imbalances there. It is a very different approach than what you have known before.

Instead of challenging the one bringing inharmony, work on the conditions that have created this in your outer reality and watch as magically you see these conditions disappear, evaporating before your eyes. This is the way of harmlessness and self mastery. This frees you from ongoing entanglements that can drain your creativity in the future. This keeps you from feeling the pain and suffering that the human selves would administer to you if you dare to expose them and bring their patterns to light. For this is the way it has ever been with human nature. Once chastised, it rises up and becomes a greater evil than it ever was before.

Instead, you can be aware and awake concerning the patterns of others, do the inner work, and allow yourself to be gently moved out of harms way. It is such a simple practice, so overlooked by humanity, who want to get into the thick of it with each other, pointing the finger of blame and thus, creating havoc in their relationships.

Another's patterns are for them to clear up in their own timing. When you are upset over another's actions, it is time for you to move into a focus of inner healing through what you are feeling, for it is within you. The upset points the way for you to turn your attention within and get to work. It alerts you to the fact that work must be done before you can return to peace, harmony, and love.

In doing this work, you may find similar triggering events on and off for a period of time. This denotes a cycle of clearing work on a specific group of patterns that are being addressed one by one. This can be profound work, healing the soul of patterns that span lifetimes and which keep bringing up reoccurring dramas in one's outer world.

For each pattern within is activated at it's appointed time and cycle and does become physical reality. Then, you must deal with the physical consequences of it. If you just ride the wave, trying to make it through the painful dramas the best you can or if you resist, finding the passage difficult, you will not have handled the core issues nor healed the pattern which means it will recycle back into your world via another scenario and this, again and again until it is healed for the last time.

If you would undo the painful aspects in your world, all the discomfort, illness, relationship issues, and hardships, you must heal the core patterns within you. There is no other way. Riding the wave of these experiences will not heal them. Diligent Inner Work will.

Be valiant, Beloved, and know it is time for great Inner Work. Exciting work, for you are being set free. I am the Inner Creative Self.

# The Magnificent Life All Souls Long For

*Awakening Soul,*
*Seek the Majestic Skies of your True Self*
*where there are no limitations, only Freedom and Peace.*

*-Babaji*

The Dream of Life is awakening into absolute freedom and peace. There is no other endeavor as worthy as the Soul seeking to know itself in its truest form, for in that one intention and focus, the Soul finds within itself all that it has ever sought in the outer world.

I am the full Magnificent Light within that is the Magnificent Life all souls long for in their inner most beings and yet, have forgotten to claim. In a world clamoring for attention, it is the rare one who seeks itself absolutely and finds the Treasure of Life.

All things have their purpose and portent, as they lead you to the Awakening. Each experience is precious in its ability to facilitate inner movement and awareness. Each encounter has a meaning and purpose. Therefore, even the least significant meetings have been Divinely Orchestrated as a means whereby the Soul can learn about its choices, momentums, and the aspects of duality that make this a unique world.

From fairer realms have you come and to these shall you return once this sojourn on Earth is over. Therefore, it behooves you to make the most of this earthly trek, to learn all things for your own advancement and growth, to soar above the seeming troubles, going deep into a learning process, which will propel you ever onward to the depths of who you are.

Know me through knowing your self in the truth of who you are. I am the Divine Principle of Being, the Transcendent One that lives forevermore in Freedom and Peace. I am Truth and a Bastion of Light so supreme, it rules galaxies of inner orbits of life intention within your soul. I am the Great Central Sun in your own inner universe. Therefore, I claim the position of your truest Light, your most Sovereign State, the truth of who you are. I am the Inner Creative Self.

# Your Eternal Freedom

*Awaken Soul, arise out of your slumber.*
*Cease to live in your prison house of flesh and earthly pursuits.*
*Reach for the star of your being, and choose to shine in a world*
*that has for too long embraced darkness as a Way of Life.*

*-Babaji*

Dearest Beloved, the moment has come for me to embrace you in the divinity you are, to carry you to new heights of transcendent awareness, which will allow you to live forever free above the clamors of the Shadowed Self. I am here this day to offer you your Eternal Freedom. Embracing my gift fully, I bring you to a whole new way of life than you have ever before imagined.

Reflect on the mastery and skill in which you have embraced virulent encounters and seeming disasters at your door. Understand with what power you wield your authority in this world and stand for peace. Reflect on the power of your Sword of Truth, which has vanquished the darkness from your being, causing it to flee. Understand the power of TheQuest Work that allows you to take dominion over situations and bring healing to the deepest levels possible within and without.

This day you can claim your True Bodhisatvahood in the Earth. You can know you are a Beneficent Light Being bringing healing to the travail of humankind, vanquishing the sorrows and pain, transforming the iniquities before you, that all who come into your presence will find mercy, healing, and peace. All will find the Sword of Truth in its fierce devotion to the True Reality and yet, will also find the compassion of a loving heart ready to embrace and heal every pattern of imperfection in this world.

I bring you glad tidings of Everlasting Joy in service to the Light, for now you have attained the inner power and equanimity that is a must for every Divine Being who walks this Earth. This day many blessings flow forth and this great wellspring of my Love and Power shall enfold you with a new sense of security and peace. I am the Inner Creative Self.

# Inner Place Prepared

*Dreams are the Visions of Spirit
drawing the Soul home to its True Abode.
They are not a call to enter the
world of form to attain worldly glories.
They beckon the Soul to greater heights of attainment,
to fairer fields of conscious realities that
far surpass the treasures one can accumulate in the Earth Realm.*

*-Babaji*

O, Beloved, Light from a distant star beckons to you, ever drawing closer and closer to your conscious reality. The Dark Night is vanquished and many demonic energies have been cleansed from the Earth body because of our work. This work, like a silent Beacon of Truth casts its shining raiment upon a darkened world and brings Light Everlasting.

You have so often forgotten to acknowledge yourself for the Light Work you do. Because of this, you have failed to see your worth in a world in travail. Your great wisdom, intelligence, insight, and love for truth has kept you apart from the world, in the sense that you have seen that dabbling with energies many engulf their lives in, believing it to be a pure and holy offering, is something to stay clear of.

Thus, the seeming rightness of ways leads souls to being immersed further in worldly energies, entangled when they could be free. Your wisdom and my Inner Guidance can keep you free and unfettered so you can live your life from a purer, freer reality than many around you have availed themselves. Thus, you can stand apart and yet, be connected.

You have felt alone in this world at times and rightfully so, for your choices have been different than many around you and your perception keener. Now is the time to come apart even further to a Place Prepared, where the silent waters waft their magic of tranquility and peace upon your psyche, where I can take the lead in your uppermost thoughts and feelings and where you can gain the ground of the Enlightened One.

Dearest Heart, the portents of the time are different for you in that they speak of surrendering the Shadowed Self as you come fully Awakened. It is a time to vanquish the darkness that has clung to the soul and claim my Eternal Freedom for the last time, for all time, forever.

This Eternal Flame radiating in your heart will assist the world far more than a dozen endeavors. This oneness of enlightened being will waft its sweet fragrance through the Earth and be felt by many souls. In the silence of your awakening, you will far more move this world into a tranquil reality than by a hundred Earth endeavors filled with personalities not attuned to my presence.

Therefore, be at peace. Allow my guidance to bring you swiftly to my Inner Abode. Honor the completeness of your present cycles and honor the many gifts that have been treasures of your heart, offerings upon the altar of life and the blessing, upliftment, and advancement of many.

You work in unseen ways. It is your greatest feat and yet, your least recognized attribute. Meditate today on the great goodness you have brought forward by this one great love to be in service to life. For in acknowledging the power of the Inner Self, you come to realize you can be anywhere and be effective in your blessing of humanity.

Now I relinquish the last vestiges of human karma from your world. Sitting on the throne of empowerment in the center of your world, I set free the Shadowed Self to soar on Wings of Light, to be all it can be, to know Eternal Freedom and Peace at last. I come with the Sword of Truth tempered by Love, a Love Supreme that casts no shadows upon the world but rather, uplifts the weary and downtrodden aspects of self to their True Estate of divine qualities and Focuses of Light.

Now everything is prepared for this great work and the place of sanctuary and peace awaits you. The Inner Self is filled with knowledge and skill that will be an exemplary partner as you traverse from the life you have known to be a citizen of Freedom and Truth.

Your True Home is calling... the inner place of Perfection and Peace. A precious home of much magnificence, beyond your imagination and dreams awaits your precious footsteps, your sweet nature, and the ancient song of your soul. It is the place where you will dream all of your highest most sacred dreams into reality. It is the place where you will be free to become the Bodhisattva, the Buddha of Bliss in its fullness, and to live in Truth, radiating that special quality into the Earth body from your place of inner peace and safety.

Tranquility and ease have been promised to you for some time. Now, in this new place you will claim it more fully and realize it as your greatest asset in coming to the full fruition of your divinity. It is in this place you will know all your prayers answered, your highest ideals realized, your greatest dreams fulfilled.

You have thought it a retreat taking you from the world and yet, you have not known the power of my presence in the world that now will be embraced by many even while you live in a retreat experience. You will see the glory of my magnificence well received in this world and sought after and you will know that your greatest destiny and glory is upon you even as you come fully awake, leading a tranquil life of blissful interactions with your angels and those of the heavens, for you are ready as you have made yourself ready to receive them.

Acknowledge your gifts this day. Drink in the praise of the Buddha Within. Bask in the splendor of your work on behalf of humanity. Know yourself as divine. Honor, accept, and love yourself as I love you and step forward free to live with me forevermore.

Relinquish the past and free yourself from entangling realities and the lifestyle of those who mean well with beautiful hearts and yet, who dabble with the Sacred Energies not knowing how much they are undoing the Sacred Matrixes their God Presence has built up as a force field of light around them.

Peace, peace, peace, Beloved. Enter now the Place Prepared, within and without. For within your heart is your inner Place of Peace, the Abode of the Buddha of Bliss, as inner and outer meet in one reality.

I am the Inner Creative Self, your God Presence, loving, supporting, and assisting your entrance into the Divine Light, which you are.

# True Freedom is Awakening to Who You Are

*Always the heart that strives for perfection does not meet its resonance in the world. The dreams and visions of the few have not found themselves in the breast of humanity. Alone, awake, aware, they have striven beyond the confines of normal earthly life, living in a realm by themselves even as they walk the Earth. It is this lonely path that has given them cause to forsake the world and to return home. For their words were not answered and their way not emulated by the vast hordes of human species, but rather scorned, adulterated, or thrown to the winds. In this one understanding they found their Truth. That one must raise their own self before they can help any others. Then, in raising Self they learn each person can only raise his or her self. In witnessing this One Truth they live free knowing all the tools, resources, availability of heavenly guides and sponsors surrounds each soul, awaiting the time when that soul will call them into action on it's ascent into its truest form. Nothing more can be done, now or forever, for it is the individual choice if he/ she will rise or fall, an individual path each one must take, individual decisions each one must make for themselves.*

*-Babaji*

O, Dearest Beloved, the Wings of Truth have singed, once again, your ideals and dreams for humanity as you have explored avenues to bring forth higher vision and awareness to this planetary realm on the eve of what could be vast destruction and the grand undoing of all that has been created before.

Know I am with you this day. As your heart saddens in its ability to effect more positive change in the world, mine becomes gladdened at the prospect of you creating your own reality as a Child of Heaven, as a Heaven born Daughter of the Light.

How much you would help humanity. How much you would raise them with your vision and help them claim a fairer world and yet, your voice rings out across a sea of asleep souls and this you have forever fought against, claiming they were ready, willing, and wanting what you could provide, what your vision could gift them and it is not true.

Humanity slumbers on the eve of probabilities of destruction, unaware and unwilling to look at what may soon come upon them. Pushing back the fear and trembling within their psyches, they fill their lives with events, dramas, and traumas to keep themselves occupied lest they, like you, become aware of what shortly must be.

Dearest Heart, the Dream for Humanity is yet to come in a future time when it can be received. The movie of life as you have witnessed it, is still very much about the Victim/Persecutors and their ever revolvement around earthly episodes that keep inflicting pain. Thus, the wars, the unconsciousness, the entrapments, and all that goes with earthly society keep people contained in a feverish nightmare that only now you have stepped free from.

For in coming apart from this society and the world at large, you have realized the futility in the game and thus, you have sought the causes and cores and found them. In finding them you have come into great wisdom and in freeing yourself, you are now out of accord with the Great Travail, which is soon upon many lives. The only True Freedom is Awakening Fully to Who You Are. The only way out of the nightmare is through the Doorway of Peace in my heart where you live in true oneness with my Divine Reality and in living free you emanate my presence into the world in a myriad of forms.

Each word, each step, each statement becomes an emanation of divinity and thus, makes its mark while you remain detached and unaffected by the choices around you. If individuals choose to rise or fall, it is not your business nor your responsibility. You cannot save them, change them, coerce them into a freer reality any more than the Heavens have been able to for centuries and eons.

So, now you understand the equation here. Now you see each one must claim freedom for themselves. Those that choose to live in unreality must make that their home for however long they can endure it until the time comes when they chafe at this reality and seek the truth within themselves, which only their God Presence can provide.

Release now your desire to help humanity, to be a servant of human beings, and live free with me, free in the inner most realms of your being, creating ever new joys within your life experience and placing yourself before any others. Not in a selfish way, but in a way of enlightened self-interest. For only you can set yourself free. All expenditure on behalf of others is a futile attempt to coerce them when they are not willing or ready to be moved.

Therefore, see this truth. Live in this reality and you will know great freedom and detachment. Those who need to drink from the well of the God Presence through the many gifts and talents you have, will find you and through their Divine Self, will tap into your precious gifts and be healed, raised, uplifted and inspired.

Tune into the gift of your Inner Work and how that work is consistent with Heaven's Will and the will of those individuals who would be cleared on deep inner levels having done the outer application. We are able to connect with their wounded aspects and do a massive healing that will deeply affect their lives in a far greater way than any outer endeavor, because the inner shifts allow a greater alignment with the God Presence, which then causes the individual's outer reality to shift to mirror that oneness. That is how life on Earth can change through the inner alignment with Spirit and thus, the outer manifestation of the God Presence and her intention for life becomes manifest.

It is so easy, so simple. No amount of talking about your vision can make a difference now, Beloved, for people are asleep and are choosing to meet life from this vantage point. There is nothing you can do but share simply with those who are awake and take your own action steps to insure your continued life of well being and ease within and without.

For understanding that it was never my will for you to suffer, you now can measure every experience to see whether it is of my will for you or your own human creation. You can heal every last schism between my Divine Intention and your creation until we align as one in intention and purpose. Then you will be done, your earthly round finished, and you will be transported to the realms where I dwell in Eternal Perfection and become one with me for all eternity, never more to return to earthly life as an Unawakened One.

Many long for your return to the Heavens, for you are loved and treasured in the realms from which you were born and have dwelled.

Now I call you home with an intensity and inner fire as strong as yours. Thus, united in purpose, the way is made clear and the fastest track to your Eternal Oneness is brought before you.

In the midst of this, last tests around planetary service from an unascended state assail you and yet, true to my Divine Intention, you swiftly move away from those energies, which would lure and court you away from accepting your full divinity in a place of retreat from the world.

The world gives its last attempt with all its greatest allure to try to take your energies and keep your focus on things that may never be given earthly circumstances. Thus have you encountered offers and open doorways and yet, now you understand open doorways to seeming great events and endeavors do not necessarily mean that Heaven has endorsed this pathway for you.

Wise and serene, you cast your attention away from the world once again, longing for my voice and I am here to guide, assist, and sponsor you, ever waiting to share my truth with you. My heart is singing with the great joy of your initiations overcome and won. Now we can turn our attention to the important issues at hand while living in sublime bliss and everlasting joy, enthusiasm, and fun.

I have told you I will take you into a whole New Life than you have yet imagined or dreamed of. Have faith and follow me unfailingly, for I shall not lead you astray. Peace, tranquility, and ease will be your lot in life despite earthly conditions, for I move you to safety, to a place where you can become fully awake without the continual allure of the outer world crashing in upon the Silent Consciousness I am giving birth to within you.

Feel the freedom of our oneness and continue to reflect on your many gifts to humanity as you have traversed this realm. Understand you are enough, you have done enough, you are doing enough, and be not dismayed when outer large projects fall away gifting you a life of greater ease, for this is my will for you. Strange as it may seem, this is the life I am leading you to.

In future time there is a convergence of souls in certain locations where a New Life is born out of the devotion to the One and alignment with certain Divine Ones that work with you there. Therefore, they have sent forth the beacon light to draw your souls to a safe abode, which they have prepared for you to make your ascension from, a place where you can draw in the richness of the True Reality, which you are, and breath out the world and its clamor, for you are being released from earthly life even as you are being initiated into Heavenly Life while on Earth. So many blessings await you, Beloved. Have faith. Believe and know Freedom and Peace.

With much Eternal Love continually flowing into your heart, mind, soul, and being, I Am the Inner Creative Self, your most Sacred God Presence.

# Release Suffering and Embrace the Path of Joy

*The Crested Jewel of my Presence
sings in your Soul.*

*-Babaji*

The Jewels of my Presence sparkle through your soul expression in a myriad of rainbow forms. I am not contained by the lesser thinking forms that have beset you, nor am I hindered in my progressive release to many worlds. I am ever free, releasing my Light throughout an Eternity of Good Will and Beneficent Activity. It is only now you are coming to understand my vastness and to anchor my presence in the mundane world in which you live.

I am forever free, sharing my Jeweled Light with many worlds in many forms. You have sought to contain my expression, not understanding I am a far vaster presence than can be contained in one medium or used for one reality.

I am Omnipresent, Omniscient, One Eternal Being that knows no containment, experiences no blocks, cannot be curtailed, contained, stopped, or extinguished. Though you have sought to destroy my essence, testing it in the waters of human experience, casting yourself in dire circumstances and allowing catastrophes and crucifixions, my Light was never altered, tainted, ruined, or destroyed, for I am indestructible.

Now that you have tested me in every way you have known possible throughout the centuries, is it not time to fully place your trust in me, to give me your full allegiance, and to be true to me as I have ever been true to you?

The simplest gift you can bestow upon me is to be fully open to my Magnificent Presence within you and to allow it to do its will on behalf of yourself, humanity, and the many worlds that float as sacred presences in a universe of sculptured light and ever-present oneness.

Gift me your full allegiance and watch as I transform your puny world of understanding and experience into a vast and magnificent wonder world where you will know continual pleasures, constant awakenings, and deep truths.

I care so much about you. I cradle you in arms of Sacred Delight. I hold you as my most Precious One. I bring you out of pain into a world of pleasure as you have never known and understood it, because you thought somehow it was wrong to feel good, to feel my presence with you. You cannot know me in pain, for pain is a foreign experience to me. You cannot find me in suffering, sorrow, sadness, or grief. Though you felt this was a worthy path that would lead to Eternal Freedom, now you see it was not. Now you can hear it from me absolutely: *There is no good reason for you to suffer in any form, for it is not and never has been my will for you.*

I live beyond suffering in a world where pleasant feelings mean oneness with God Essence, where pleasure is not a sin nor a deviance of the Path, but a true and rightful place to seek God. What do you feel in nature? A sense of peace, well being, ease, and rapture. This rapture is the Essence of God, the God Presence within you. This nature experience leads you into the rapture of the Holy Spirit within you and therefore, this rapturous, pleasurable experience is a route to Divine Union.

Many years ago in centuries past, you were told with humanity pleasure was of the Devil and a sin, when in truth, pain is of the dark side, the Shadowed Self, and is never known in Divine Realities. All suffering ceases when one traverses the higher realms where the Presence of God is known within every soul and where life is lived from that One Eternal Reality.

Meditate upon my words and know that this is truth. Pleasure equals closeness to God. Pain equals closeness to the Shadow Self. There must then be a rerouting of your thinking processes to envelop this new concept and to allow yourself to live out of this new reality.

Try it out and see how in seeking pleasure and pleasurable experiences, you are more in touch with God, more in communion with me than ever before, and then make your choice. Then choose whether you will perpetuate suffering and pain in your reality anymore and if this can have any value or worth for you as a life experience.

When you move out of the Way of Suffering as a Life Path, you enter the Path of Joy, where all wholesome pleasures are known as a way to experience God in the feeling and physical worlds. What a different reality than what has been taught. What an imperfect world was created by this one attachment to a belief that was never passed down by Christ or any other Master.

How the world has waxed strong in its painful attitudes and experiences that bring suffering at every turn. How filled is this world with suffering souls rather than joy filled beings. This misqualified life, this whole miscreation can be traced to the belief that somehow it is sinful to feel good, to revel in beneficent feelings, to enjoy pleasurable moments, and to bask in the goodness that God has gifted every soul.

Instead, the world has darkened and everywhere there is suffering and pain. Everywhere there is shadow and darkness, because pain is of the darkness. It is a shadowed aspect that is a quality of human creation rather than divine.

There is nothing beneficial in suffering except the learning and growth given to the Soul that teaches it the difference between the Rapture of God and Glory of the Heaven Worlds, and the pain of the Shadowed Self and the density of the Earth Realms.

This is an important teaching and well worth clearing within of any beliefs still attached to suffering and pain as a way of life. It is time to step completely free and to live in Eternal Joy and Prosperity with me.

I love, bless, honor, and adore you. I treasure you and would shower you with millions of pleasurable experiences all geared to bring you into complete union and oneness with me. I am the Ever-present One within you, the Inner Creative Self.

# Awakening to Your True Divine Purpose

Life in all its splendor can never compare to the Glorious Life that awaits the Soul's return into its True Estate. Beyond the farthest reaches of humanity's highest goals and dreams lies a garden of such transcendent beauty and awe inspiring magnificence, the Soul who finds it trembles with delight. It is here, beyond dream and vision, where True Reality lies. It is this goal of goals, this last endeavor, which propels the Soul to its Eternal Freedom, opening the gates of Eden at last.

Seek not the dream in this world, nor cling to things that seem normal, comfortable, and safe, for these will keep you ever tied to the rebirth and death cycle of the Earth. Instead cast your dreams to the wind and stand alone upon the mountain top calling in your Truest Self, your True Reality and watch how the mirage of life dissipates before your eyes, leaving only that which resonates with your new awareness of Truth.

Then climb on through the inner ladder of Self Realization until you have won your complete freedom, nevermore turning your eyes back to the worldly occupations that once looked awesome and powerful in their ability to touch many lives.

Instead, claim Freedom and live in Truth. Be free and know in your freedom you silently call to thousands if not millions of souls to follow you. It is the highest occupation and service you can render humanity. For a soul becoming free sends out its rare vibration into the airwaves of the Earth and on the ethers wafts its sweet fragrance of the Enlightened Awakening One.

The power and magnitude of this Presence in the Earth is beyond comparison with any known earthly occupation, no matter how vibrant, outstanding, and spectacular. Thus, the Wise One understands the futility of earthly offices and opens fully to the Winds of Freedom that waft gently upon the Soul, calling it home to Paradise.

-Babaji

Miracles upon miracles abound as you, my Beloved, cease to dwell in worldly consciousness, seeking the peace and freedom of my presence. The dreams of your life are now resolved and with their release you will find a whole new reality and perspective awakening within you.

You will see the valiant efforts of many angels, elementals, and precious Souls of Light continually bringing beneficent energies to the Earth. You will see how full is this world of heavenly bodies resonating with the highest keynotes and frequencies, ever wafting their sweet essences among peoples, projects, countries, and activities, raising, uplifting, and inspiring. To see this is to set yourself free to become a God Free Being at last, understanding that Earth and its habitants are well cared for.

Now is the time to raise your sights upon goals and dreams of a higher nature, to follow your heart where your greatest service and commitment is calling you. This is beyond the normal simple earthly life of an Earth Inhabitant, catapulting you into Heavenly Realms with heavenly missions that far surpass all that you have endeavored to gift the people here.

This is not a shrugging off of responsibilities nor turning your back upon a world in need. Rather, it is the awakening into your True Reality, your true Divine Purpose and true Mission.

You are one of many destined to ascend in this lifetime and this is the greatest gift your soul can offer humanity at this time. All other gifts are far lesser manifestations of Heaven's Love.

The greatest love is to show the way by making the Ascension the heart's first desire and our union the uppermost ideal and goal of your life. With this one thing comes a thousand footsteps, easily and gracefully making their way to complete freedom and that is where life truly begins.

What you believed was life, in all its entrapments, glamour, and schemes, will suddenly pale before your view of the New Reality your Soul has entered into. You will look back and laugh at the disfigurement of all your dreams, hopes, and desires for the Earth, for you will understand what truly is and what is destined to be, and how far earthly reality is from that perspective at this point in time.

You were not meant to suffer nor to be in the Great Travail, overcome and banished from the Light of Heavenly Kingdoms. You are meant to rise on Wings of Light and Freedom, to dwell in Everlasting Peace and Hope, and to know yourself fully and absolutely as divine and this Life is calling you to.

All those Blessed Ones who surround you with their love and wisdom, enfolding your life and keeping you safe as you blossom fully and become fully realized, remain beside you to walk this last pathway with you to Eternal Freedom.

It is a blessed day that has cast out the shadows from your heart and lifted the veil from your mind. You will see truly and absolutely, and these new views will astound you. You will set foot upon the Divine Reality within the Divine Life, which is True Sacred Living, and you will know Peace, Prosperity, Tranquility, and Ease as you enter a time of great wealth and advancement for your Soul.

I now cloth you in wealth and splendor and ask that you remain in gratitude accepting my Divine Gifts, understanding it is for your highest good to experience this level of wealth and magnificence before your Ascension in the Light. For it will wipe away all the beliefs that once held you in poverty on Earth, and it will assist others to claim their Divine Inheritance as well within a sacred spiritually devoted life. Therefore, open up heart and hands to now receive my outpouring, for the spring has dashed forth from the mountain of my presence and a mighty River of Gold is pouring forth into your hands and use today.

In this next cycle, there is much outpouring of wealth and much activity in securing the Inner Place Prepared. Amidst this important cycle is your continued edification as a Soul of Great Light through the Inner Work and meditations. These must remain first and foremost during this time for me to be able to pour into your life all I would.

Dearest One, this release will be the greatest joy and most magnificent outpouring in your earthly life. Enjoy it fully and live in the joy and magic it brings. For it is Heaven's gift to a world awakening and it is a gift to your soul to receive and be the vessel of so great a light and healing outpouring.

Joy, joy, joy is your keynote now, joy in Everlasting Life. Be prepared, for many earthly changes are catapulting you into your New Life. Understand the blessings that are there for you as I prepare your safe abode for the next cycle.

Live in Peace, dwell in Tranquility. Journey to the Higher Realms and learn that your truest friends are there. Seek not earthly pleasures that are dissipating, but focus on the pleasures of Spirit. Those experiences will enhance your love of the Divine Life with those you have come to know as friends and sponsors who are ever with you, uplifting your life to new heights you cannot even imagine, so wondrous are they.

Now Elohim gift you as wealth descends and a new world calls to you, a new understanding and a new perspective that allows you to release all attachments to earthly life and live free.

I am the Inner Creative Self reveling in the joy of your awakening and the vast freedom that has been imparted to you this day through Elohim. Live in Gratitude and know how much you are loved.

# Gifts From the Heavens Descend in a River of Gold

*The Rapture of Heaven's Embrace is an incomparable experience.*
*To the world traveler, it is a Beacon of Hope, a Place of Refuge,*
*a retreat from the storm of earthly existence and karmic recompense.*
*It is the Dream of dreams, the ideal of each and every*
*Saint and Sage who has walked this Earth.*
*It is the promise to all who come to hold it as the greatest treasure,*
*the most sought after jewel, the one indistinguishable union*
*that surpasses all others and which gives the soul its Eternal Freedom.*
*Seek ye first this Heavenly Experience and*
*all things will be added unto you.*

*-Babaji*

Beloved, the Divine welfare from which I draw my ever present good and work it on your behalf is now opening wide its gates to flood into your world with boundless wealth, unimaginable opulence, and a tranquility and ease you have never known except in the Heaven Realms.

This gift from those on high, who have watched your progress and are in full support of your work and destiny on behalf of this planet, have decided your wealth now be magnified to match your diligence in planetary service and that nothing be held back.

Now the elementals gather and you wonder why. For the action of the elementals is very blessed in their ability to anchor light in the Earth and with that, create nature in its most awesome beauty, perfect weather, perfect harmony, radiating the Light Eternal into the souls of humanity.

So it is with the Devic Kingdom, who are now in service en mass on your behalf, who have come to witness the great outpouring of light into your world in a River of Gold, and who have aligned to assist you in anchoring wealth, prosperity, and ease on every level, creating within your force field a Golden Age Environment that far surpasses anything you have yet created on Earth in many lives.

Therefore, they herald in the Great Light that surpasses all understanding, and which will quickly catapult you and your beloveds into a whole new reality and way of living.

For Opulence and Wealth opens many doors. It is right upon you. I tell you this so you learn to trust my word absolutely, so you will know that when I speak, it is in Truth, which I love. I am the Inner Creative Self.

# You Rule Supreme in Your World

*Peace in all its Splendor and Magnificence*
*has chosen to dwell in the heart of the Compassionate Chela*
*whose dedication, purity, and purpose is aligned with the I Am,*
*and whose intention for complete union is first and foremost in her life.*
*Thus, Peace comes to grace her life in a most powerful way,*
*emanating out to greet many souls upon the path and*
*ignite their own Quest for Eternal Oneness.*

*-Babaji*

Beloved, how long have I traversed the Heaven Realms beckoning for you to meet me in the place of absolute joy. How much fun I would bring to your life should you relinquish past patterns of sternness, seriousness, and solemnness. How ever-present I am to gift you Harmony and Love, Tranquility and Ease and a sense of the Wondrousness and Magic of Life that abounds all around you.

Yes, the planet converges to meet many karmic patterns and outcomes, and yes these are serious times. Nevertheless, in the midst of travail there is a Place of Peace, an Inner Sanctuary of Absolute Beauty and Magnificence where the Soul can abide in tranquil reflection, free from the solemnity of the world and its earthly condition.

This place is where I dwell and the more you visit me here, the more you wrap yourself in my peace, freedom, and loveliness that far surpasses beauty in any present form you know.

How much I would gift you and how often you hold me back. Just when I think you will engage with me in Everlasting Joy, patterns arise to keep you in the confines of the serious nature, which is my antithesis. For I am a Child of Joy and Woman of Absolute Freedom. I am the all encompassing River of Gold pouring its magnificent light into your world, hoping you will gift yourself with that which I have intended for you.

Forever it is and ever it shall be... *You rule supreme in your world.* If you would have me rule, take command and make all things right, then you must relinquish the patterns that have forever held me back and pushed me out of the inner throne of your being.

This Place of Power has been usurped by patterns and beliefs contrary to the Will of Heaven for you, which would shower you with all perfection, harmony, prosperity, and peace.

You have believed other things. You have thought of God as a stern father who withholds, sends blights, and creates imperfection to punish an erring humanity. That which you shrink from is not the Father God, who emanates only perfection and therefore cannot create anything less, but the Inner Stern Father you have set up as your God.

Now, understanding this equation, you will see how this one image and the beliefs around it have caused much havoc in your consciousness, being, and world. For it is truly the antithesis of all that is true and real in the Heaven Planes.

Thus, a life of hardship and struggle has ensued with the idea the hard Taskmaster God is ever peering down at your iniquities, forever displeased. With this concept, one can never enter the joy of their own beingness, loveliness, and perfectness, but only suffer on, never feeling adequate, never understanding they are enough, never being able to please this unpleasable stern and strict father.

The statement: "God has send his wrath upon the world," is a misunderstanding of the Laws of Life and Heaven. For God in its infinite mercy, compassion, and peace never sends out anything but Harmony, Love, and Perfection.

It is humankind who have created the lesser images, filled a world with imperfection, and then made themselves victims to their own creation. In their pain and suffering, they cry out to God for mercy, when in truth it is to themselves they must appeal and then with diligence, route out the patterns that have forever created imperfectly causing them great harm.

It is time for humanity to cease their childish ways and ignorant conceptions, become Masters of their Fate, stepping forth to heal their misconceptions and miscreations, take responsibility for the state of the world and why it is so much less than the Perfect Plan and beautiful

Eden created by God. It is time for humankind to release themselves from sorrow, suffering, and pain as a way of life, and to fully embrace the Divine Life and Divine Inheritance that is God's Will for them.

I am forever holding you in my Divine Embrace, sharing with you the Sweet Nectar of Divine Bliss, and longing for you to realize me fully. Through Self Realization you become free, fully accepting your divinity as your Divine Birthright and relinquishing the hold the human self has kept upon you for millennia.

Today I live in great joy knowing you are choosing to align with me fully, heal past beliefs that have kept their stranglehold of imperfection in your world, wake up to who you truly are, and feel my full presence with you always.

So many gifts I am now pouring into your world. Know the joy and Sweet Nectar of Divine Bliss as the ecstatic ministry of my presence. I love and adore you, my Precious One. I am the Inner Creative Self, the Mighty I Am.

# You Are an Instrument

*Life, Eternal, Vibrant, and Alive, is ever present within you.*
*Anything less is of the human creation.*

*-Babaji*

Beloved One, the strains of the Heavenly Symphony move through your being, now attuned and attuning to the Divine Frequencies. You are an instrument through which Divine Melodies are played by the Divine One, which I Am.

Each season has its theme, as does each moon cycle, each week and day. Thus, each quality is an essence or vibration corresponding to a sound. The blend of God Qualities in a day, ever changing and interchanging to create melodies among themes, send forth their vibrations into the world, resounding in a full symphony of vibration resulting in the emanation of many qualities.

Mixes of hope, love, purity, courage, and peace send forth an uplifting energy to the world, while anger, upset, and frustration sends forth darkness and despair. *"Lord, make me an instrument of Thy Peace,"* is a call to be a Vessel of Divine Frequencies rather than human creations.

Precious is your light this day, your fragrance and radiance wafting on the airwaves of this Earth. As you consecrate your Sacred Temple within and without, you enter the Sacred Life.

Thus, each moment you live in sanctification, a Holy One in the Earth allowing the Symphony of God Qualities to be played through your temple and thereby, living as a saint in the Earth, you exemplify Sacred Living.

This day I bless you abundantly that every dream of your heart be realized in these days to come as you sanctify your every moment by my Divine Inspiration and Intention for your life. I love and bless you. I am the Inner Creative Self.

# There is No Judgment of Your Soul

*Trust in the Divine Principles you base your life on,*
*and know they will set you free.*
*The Freedom you seek is but a few steps away,*
*steps into the Eternal Light and Oneness,*
*into the Truth of who you are.*
*As you set your course for living in*
*absolute oneness with your Divine Self,*
*forevermore relinquishing the hold*
*the Shadowed Self has had on you,*
*you enter what is called the Divine Life.*
*This is the Bastion of Freedom that has embraced*
*each stalwart soul who has made the trek*
*before you to their True Self.*

*-Babaji*

Beloved One, the answer to all your questions and prayers is in the sheltered abode of the Bodhisattva Within. In this Magnanimous Heart dwells all the power, transcendent wisdom, and benevolent intention your soul could ever know.

The Truth lies within you. All that you seek is there for you. There is not one person outside of yourself that can give you the full view of who you are, but rather portions of the self, which is too vast for anyone's sight on Earth.

In your divinity, you are a vast and powerful being. In your Truth, you have no shadowed awareness, no regrets or losses, no pain or suffering. The Eternal Being, which you are, dwells in absolute perfection in the higher planes while the soul body in which you travel, traverses many realities and must choose, moment by moment, which it will dwell in.

In the Earth Plane you are given Heaven and Hell as choices of a life experience. You are allowed the full exploration of these realms with no judgment. You have traversed both in very extensive life experiences and still my love for you remains unchanged and unmoved, no matter what you have passed through.

In the Highest Realms, where only perfection is known, there is no judgment of your soul and no awareness you must atone err you return home. This concept is of the limited shadowed self who views all it has passed through as wrong or bad and which carries a heavy load of judgment for experimenting with darkness, in dark thoughts and feelings, in unkind acts and ignorant deeds, in evil intentions and actions.

In the realms where I dwell in absolute purity and freedom, there is no judgment for this experiment and experience. In knowing this, you can set yourself free from the pain and sorrow deep in your soul for what you have viewed as transgressions to life and you can return home to the safe abode of Eternal Freedom.

Forever you have kept your soul locked in earthly rounds of embodiment, never feeling pure and whole enough to return to the realms from whence you came, which is your True Home.

A whole Astral Plane had to be created for you and others, who not believing in yourself and your innate goodness, purity, and wholeness, relegated yourself to planes where imperfection and inharmony still reign. Even the highest realms of this astral plane are but a paltry resemblance of the Heaven Realms from which you were born and now must return as an Eternal Spirit.

There have been many experiments on Earth and your soul has grown full with them. Now it understands the duality of this plane and the consequences of certain soul actions and beliefs. It has gotten a greater education than it ever could have received by any other experience, because it was able to step into the experiment fully, live it lifetime after lifetime, and play it out in so many different scenarios, seeking always to know what would be the outcome and finding those outcomes absolutely.

Now you would come home. You have believed your trek of many lifetimes is unforgivable and an abomination of desolation that has marked your soul forever and yet, it is not true. You are Heaven Born. You chose to descend to Earth and experience many things. Within the framework of this earthly experience, you made many choices and had many outcomes and some of these caused great pain and suffering. Thus you learned what works and what does not work for you, what serves and what does not. You have grown in compassion for the plight of others and the love in your heart has expanded and radiated its sweet essence in this world.

Now you seek freedom and I am that Freedom. I am the choice of choices. When you choose me in any given moment in time, you choose the Divine Reality. You choose Truth, Purity, Beauty, Wholeness, and Peace. It is as simple as that, making moment-to-moment choices to dwell in my oneness, to live by Love, to send forth radiant energies of beautiful God Qualities that grace your soul and give you edification.

You choose Light and Light descends. You move away from the Shadowed Self and see it in all its limiting beliefs and ways of being, and you know this way no longer serves you. You embrace this part of yourself and bring healing, transformation, and peace to its many aspects.

Each healing and clearing sets you freer and freer as you raise your vision to the Heaven Realms and draw from the Divine Elixir of Life to sustain you, fortify you, and carry you forward on the momentum you have built, healing every last vestige of the Shadowed Self that you may become Free.

I am here to share with you this day... *Your Freedom is at hand.* Each moment you choose my light, awareness, and truth, you are claiming this freedom in your soul. Each clearing, where you work lovingly with the Shadowed Parts of self, you move into the Light Eternal and dwell there for longer and longer periods.

This is the Way of Truth, the Way of Freedom every soul who has won their freedom walked before you. Whatever methodology they used to overcome the Shadowed Self and transform its energies back into the Divine Essence was unique to them. Each one had to face and conquer aspects of self to be truly free. They had to face, overcome, and move away from the shadow way of being, claiming their True Reality and their True Self as the only power in their world. Thus, they won the day.

We have magnificent examples in this world of many souls who made the climb into their True Self and chose to live eternally in the oneness of their True Reality. This magnificent experience awaits you as one of many choices on this Earth. Each day you can choose to live in this reality, moving from its Divine Essence into Shadowed Awareness where there is work to be done to facilitate healing in the Inner Kingdoms.

You have walked this path most valiantly and I commend you for your courage and willingness to go all the way in winning your Eternal Freedom. That which you seek shall be found. That which you choose shall be, for on Earth your will is supreme. There is great power in clear intentions and great momentum in your will and direction. For all the universe rushes to serve you in outplaying that which you intend to be your reality.

I am the Supreme Being living in Eternal Oneness. I dwell in Heaven Realms and anchor myself in your soul as you command me. I am in all places in your reality when you choose to give me the power in your world. When you dethrone the Shadowed Self, relegating it to healing and transformation rather than ruling your world, you give me my sacred position in your life to bring forth perfection and a paradise beyond what you could ever imagine.

Now I share with you one more truth. It is this... the outer world is a mirror of your Inner Reality. Even as your nation continues to put those in power as their president who dwell not from the Inner Light, and other nations do the same, it is a significant sign that collectively people are choosing to enthrone the Shadowed Self in the most Holy Place within, the place of absolute power in their worlds.

When souls awaken and reinstate the God Presence in this most sacred of places within, you will see a wholly different government and a completely elevated society in all its many manifestations.

Thus, the Soul can see any earthly condition and look deep within to find the same reality there. The key then is in clearing these conditions within, healing and transforming them that the Light Eternal may ever be present, radiant, and alive within you. I am the Inner Creative Self.

# Life is an Adventure in Awakening

*The finite reality can never fully express nor
experience the Divine Reality.
Therefore, it is not about embracing or
encompassing the Divine Self from the Lesser Self
but rather, a dissolving of the Lesser Self
in the vast all encompassing Divine Presence.*

*-Babaji*

My Beloved, Dearest of my Heart, life is an incredible journey, an Adventure in Awakening and with it, so many ideals realized and depth discovered as you traverse the Inner Self with all its realities, discerning and discovering which are Divine and which are finite, as the Master has said.

In understanding both are housed within your consciousness, within your psyche, you become the Master of your Fate as you weed out every last vestige of the Unreal Self and discover instead, the truth of who you are.

For each place you have held an unreal belief about yourself, is a station that has locked unreality into your life experience. This unreality has lent to many experiences and expressions of your self that have not been true to who you really are.

Many on this planet are so immersed in the Unreal Self, they have no idea a Divine Self even exists. So caught up in earthly life and human momentums, they live life from a limited reality, never dreaming of the freedom that exists right within their grasp and right within their own being. All it takes is intention, a clear intention to be free, to step forward as their True Self, live out of their True Identity, and cast into the flame all impostors of who they really are.

Beloved, the Impostors must go, err you are free. Not in a way of annihilation as some have so abstractly put it, causing more and more schisms in their psyches but rather, an embracing and compassionate understanding of the many aspects of self causing limitation in your world, that have caused hardship, suffering, pain, lack, and frustrations of every kind. All these things must be healed with their causes and cores, for they are the antithesis of my will for you and Heaven's intention for your life.

How far beyond the limitations of your understandings, beliefs, and life expression are the True Divine Qualities, which embody the truth of who you are. How wondrous is it to see you so focused and intent upon awakening fully to this Divine Reality, putting behind you the Sleep of Ages and the walk through turmoil and travail the Human Self created.

Now it is time for becoming fully awake, aware, and for living in your wisdom, your ever-present Wise Self, which I am. Beyond every limited understanding, unknowing, conflict, or confusion, I remain available for you to access my true assessment of your life's path.

How often I would gift you this knowledge, this depth of understanding, while you pass moments and hours wrestling with doubts and fears unwarranted and unnecessary. For you have believed this to be an evil world where life is against you. Out of many sorrows and suffering, you have come to believe it is hard here, one must struggle to make it through, pass through hardship and pain to be free. This is all untrue and simply a way of seeing life, which then creates life after its image and yet, was never my intention for you for one moment.

Understand this and begin to bask in the ever-present beneficent energies constantly around you, assisting you, and moving you towards your Divine Reality. There is so much goodness in this world, so many beautiful beings from the Masters to Angels to the Devic Kingdom and Elemental worlds, all holding for you in the highest, who are there for you every moment of the day to lend their wisdom, enlightenment, assistance, caring, and direction, and who delight each time you open to their presence and love.

I am ever present with you, guiding you into your True Reality, helping you on all levels to become the Free Being you really are, and helping you make wise choices every step of the way as you minister to yourself and the Inner Kingdom of aspects, healing and transforming each one that is a lesser image than who you are, each belief that would bind you rather than set you free.

Know my presence with you and have faith in good things to come. The world prepares for many more calamities and upset, a Grand Travail on many levels experienced by all. In the midst of this time, I am here to set you free, to awaken you fully that you may take your place as an Ascended Master in the Highest Order forever free.

This is my intention and my will for you. As you align your intentions and will with mine, magic happens. There is a great acceleration beyond what you have imagined possible. Trust and remain one pointed and all things will unfold easily and effortlessly with great joy carrying you forward to victory upon victory. I am the Inner Creative Self.

# Open Your Eyes to the Ever Present Wonder

*The Trek of the Awakening Soul is one*
*that is unique unto itself.*
*There are no guidelines nor guideposts that truly fit,*
*for each Soul is unique and therefore*
*must walk its own original path to its unfoldment.*
*No one can set the course for another,*
*nor know absolutely what is the right thing for that one.*

*-Babaji*

Beloved One, the brilliant day calls out its mysteries to you. The laughing clouds, light, luminescent and free, birds in flight, butterflies, dragonflies, fragrant flowers blowing in the wind, rainbows brilliant across the mountain tops. All these things call to your attention and are there for your enjoyment and enrichment.

Each day casts its fragrant wonders before you and you, the ever developing Soul, traverse time and space either attuned to the brilliant display of a glorious nature wonderland before you or immersed in thoughts and feelings that keep you enveloped and therefore separate from the lovely world around you.

Peace, tranquility, ease, joy, enthusiasm, playfulness, and tenderness all can be found in nature, reflecting the Divine Inner Creative Self, which I Am. All these Divine Qualities are forever parading before you, enticing you to come play, be alive, feel free, sing deeply, share profoundly with the Nature Spirits who fill every land.

Joy is the keynote of the divine aspects of nature. Joy travels through the airwaves of Earth, trumpeting its presence, its divine eloquence before the busy worlds of humanity and who stops to listen? Who stops to play? Who stops to dance with the beauty of nature, to sing with the glory of the skies, to gallop through the flower filled fields of Nature's Glory?

Today, stop to reflect on the vast array of perfection before you that comes through the Elemental Kingdom and that everywhere surrounds you in nature. View the magnificent artwork of the Great Master, the Divine Presence at work behind each beautiful flower and blessed creature. Drink in the Glorious Day and the star filled night and know life is wondrous, profound, sacred, enchanting, and magical. Through the serene reflection of Nature, the Soul can find peace and move into a life filled with tranquility and ease, laughter and fun, perfection and grace.

Nature's abundance shows that the Divine One who dwells within the Souls of Humanity is Abundant, loves Opulence, basks in Wealth, knows only Perfection, Beauty, and Wondrousness. Where Nature is allowed its perfect course, perfection reigns. Where man has tampered with natural forces, one finds a very different reality, a mirror to the inner workings of a forgetful soul who in the midst of Divine Beauty, Opulence, and Wealth, chooses to slumber and in its slumber, to dream a different reality, a reality of lack and limitation, of a world where there is not enough and where Nature, once beautiful and profound, turns into an ugly creature bringing danger and destruction.

Today I call you to heal the dream that has cast its shadows upon a world creating the Great Travail. Today I call you to release beliefs that you deserve lack and discomfort in any form. Today I ask you to believe in yourself as a Divine Being come to experience life on Earth, to love yourself and your divinity with all the energy you can muster. When you love yourself truly, you will gift yourself the original Divine Intention that prevails and did prevail before the Dream, which ever awaits your entrance back into its Splendorous Garden, where only that which will bless, nurture, and fulfill you resides.

Today I ask you to open your eyes to the ever-present Oneness and Truth that is everywhere around you, that lives in every flower and tree, sings out to you from each blossom and cloud, calls to your inner senses, drawing you into a world of happiness, fulfillment, and joy, that has as its one intention, to bless you, nourish you, and fill your life with exquisite wondrousness.

Laugh, play, feel alive, be free. Turn the tides of the ancient dream that says one must suffer here. Claim Heaven in your own life experience and trade the dream in for the True Reality of your Divine Oneness with all life. Cherish the blessed gifts that pour forth in abundance to you each day and live eternally happy and free in the Garden of Life that ever was, is, and ever will be around you. I Am the Inner Creative Self.

# Finding the Lost Chord of Your Divine Self

*Invincible, dynamic, and absolute in its statement of truth,*
*the Divine Self remains ever the herald of what is to come.*
*In its pristine purity, it launches its Divine Will*
*simply and absolutely, moment by moment,*
*only to be deterred by the willful Soul.*
*Through the surrender of personal will, this dynamic will*
*casts its perfect creation from its own Innate Authority,*
*releasing the Divine Blueprint for the Soul.*
*Ever creating in perfection, the Soul enters a reality*
*unlike what it has known in the Earthly Realm,*
*for the Garden reappears and bids him/her enter.*
*It is then the Divine Intention is manifest in all its*
*fullest import and innovation and the*
*Soul is released from the bonds of iniquity and travail.*

*-Babaji*

My Precious One, it is a joy to witness your deep clearings that give me full expression through you and the ability to live fully expressing my freedom and truth. I acknowledge you this day for your dedication to the Divine Perfection, which is the completeness that I am.

You can think of the Soul in its trek through time as incomplete, seeking its Lost Chord. It enters the world and then quickly forgets its Divine Heritage and its union with God. Instead, it begins to experience itself as separate, alone, without, and somehow lacking the knowledge, ability, and skills to recreate the Divine Perfection, which is innate within its nature.

Thus, alone in the world, it begins to seek for truth and the other lost part of itself. It experiences the repercussions of life lived from separateness and unreality while striving to find itself within the maze of life. The more fire and determination in the Soul, the more dedicated and committed it is to awakening the lost parts of itself and finding its truth at last.

Meanwhile, other souls might choose to glide through many lifetimes content with the explanations of life other lost souls might give them. Lost, meaning unknown to itself, not knowing its origin or where it came from, its purpose or intention.

After many rounds of rebirth and trial and error methods of bringing forth satisfactory results in relationships, business, and health, the Soul begins to seek the truth of its existence and remove itself from those limiting beliefs that have kept it feeling lost and alone.

The coldness of the world lends its magic, for the Aspiring Soul must ever climb into higher awareness seeking the way out, the truth of its existence, and who it is in its truest sense. Then, the miracles begin pouring forth as memories return. The Soul sees truth and understands the reason behind such a journey and the travail it has met along the way.

Now, with fire and fervor, it unhooks itself from chords unseen that have bound it through the ages and propels itself into clarity and truth. No longer happy with the explanations of other lost souls, meaning ones who have forgotten who they are, the Soul ceases to be led down life's highways by those who cannot remember any more than they.

Instead, it searches the histories to see if there have been any others who have sought truth and awakened to who they really are, who have remembered and in their remembering have stepped free from the entangled life that holds all souls in its web.

It learns there is a purpose behind the trials and it must give up everything to remember, every drive, intention, desire, wish and all willing to a higher more knowledgeable power. For until it does, it will never cease to travel Earth's highways propelling itself into more and more entangling affairs.

The Limited Soul cannot know the greater way that is there for it. It must find its Lost Part, the part that remembers and knows all. It must be led by the one that can see, rather than others who are traversing the Dark Night, blind and out of touch with who they are. It must take the hand of the Knowing Self and be drawn swiftly and absolutely into the

Light Eternal, into the daylight of comprehension and knowing. Then, and only then, will it be free.

The wondrousness of this passage can be likened to a prisoner of lifetimes, living in a dark cell with dark creatures, being released into the light of day to live as a Free Being. The difference between the earthly unconscious life and the life of truth and freedom is like the difference between a dark and limiting cell and the beautifully sculptured landscape of a heavenly garden scene.

There is no comparison and yet, souls are content to live in the darkness, never striving to know who they are or from whence they have come, what they can really do and accomplish, and where they are bound. For this is the Mystery of Life and yet, how many raise their heads to seek and then find? A few valiant souls here and there?

Now understand my gratitude for your unswerving devotion to truth. Now realize how powerful a time you have entered, where I am able to greet you, converse with you, and gift you your every dream and desire because you have surrendered your will to me and allowed my will to rule supreme in your temple and being.

I am the way of the True Life. As you embrace me and enter this most Sacred Holy Offering with me, the world is transformed. For you no longer witness it as you have in the past. Your sight is cleared and you view all things in the truth they are or with the compassionate understanding of what they could be. Never in judgment nor sorrow over choices because you realize the Divine Reality, each soul governs his/her world and each is learning, growing, and educating himself/herself.

It is not for you or anyone to remove this grand opportunity for exploration into the Shadowed Self and the shadowed life anymore than anyone has tampered with your soul, making it unfree to do what it will. For this is true unconditional loving, true freedom, and that is God.

I am the Inner Creative Self, your champion and administrator. In love and blessings, I greet you and stand with you forever in the Light.

# Blessing of Christmastide

*Ingenious and willing is the Divine Self*
*to offer every opportunity for advancement and growth.*
*The greatest achievements and attainments are truly the*
*gifts of this Divine part of ourselves.*
*Nothing blesses our world that does not come from this Presence.*
*No glory, no success, no fulfillment in its truest sense arrives without*
*being from the will and intention of the Divine Self in action.*
*Therefore, the world cannot and never will of itself*
*gift us that which the Indwelling Presence has designed for us.*
*Neither should we waste time or effort in gaining the*
*things of this world as a means to fulfill and*
*satisfy a part of ourselves that has lost sight of the Presence.*
*For true fulfillment, accomplishment, and satisfaction are a*
*result of a unity with the Divine Self and from that oneness,*
*its expression in our outer world.*
*Therein lies the True Path to Joy and Fulfillment,*
*the true interest that must attend the Stalwart Soul.*

*-Babaji*

Great joy abounds, Beloved, as Christmas Angels and Devas attend thee. How grateful am I to see the joy expressing through you, my will and intention for this sacred period of your life. You are rising up and claiming it with a full heart, mind, and soul, receptive, open, and willing, which allows My Presence to be fully with you.

It is during the Sacred Days ahead you shall learn the true meaning of Christmastide. For it is a time for souls enmass to awaken and emulate the Christic Flame within, radiate to everyone they meet this Christ Presence, and be as a mighty wave and tide of light emanation, bathing the planet and starry bodies beyond with the glorious Christ Mass Presence. This is unique to this planet, a gift from the Blessed Jesus and his family, that those on Earth may understand and embrace the Christ Flame within themselves, and in renewing and reigniting this spark within them each Christmas, will learn to live from this Christ Presence each and every day of their lives.

For in the joy abounding at this time, when angels are everywhere and elemental life are singing hosannas of joy, the Earth enters a time of sacred home life, where altars made from fragrant trees are set up in every home, reflections of the Divine Presence within and the many God Qualities that are the Divine Nature of each one. These fragrant and precious altars waft their sweet essence upon the minds and hearts of humanity, quickening within them the joyfulness of true sharing and giving, which is of the Nature of God and qualities of their True Natures.

A stillness enters the Earth and with it, a time of quiet joy and fulfillment, laughter and fun. It is a time of song and dance, of Divine Recreation as many come to celebrate the Christ in their own unique way. Even unto the most unaware soul, the essence of Christ-Mass-Tide floods forth its presence and is heard and understood in the deepest most sacred parts of self.

Joy, Joy, Joy is abounding this Christmastide, as more souls are awakened to the Divine Presence within. As they gift others and enter true selflessness, thinking how to please and bring joy, they enter a self-less service focused for a time on the happiness of those around them, rather than on themselves. Creating a magical fairyland of Christmas focuses throughout homes and offices, workplaces and buildings, and Christmas altars, which are the Christmas trees full of beauty, splendor, and light, the deeper meaning sinks into the minds of humanity. It seeps into the senses and creates a profound awakening, transformation, and healing. For even when Christmas triggers sorrow, it is cleansing and purifying the soul, making it ready for the New Year, the new opportunity to live from the Christ Love that each person felt during Christmastide.

Someday in the not so distant future, humankind will celebrate Christmas everyday. Not in its present form, but in the wondrousness of the Christ Light emanating from each Awakened Soul who dwells on Earth. In that time, beautiful altars will be everywhere and will remain all year round, and Sacred Living will be a Way of Life that is embodied by all. I am the Inner Creative Self, blessing you in this most Sacred Christ Mass Tide.

# I Am the Way to Safety Serenity and Ease

*When the journey's end is in sight,*
*the Soul on its Sacred Pathway sees a Great and Luminescent Light.*
*As it draws near, it catches sight of a Divine Image that*
*is a profound reflection of its truest Self.*
*Thus, the last steps are fulfilled,*
*as the Soul merges on the Pathway of Life with its Divinity.*

*-Babji*

My Dearest One, as you sit in your lonely laboratory pondering choices and the time ahead, consider this: *Life is an accumulation of past momentums mixed with the amount of Divine input allowed at a given time.* Therefore, as you open your soul more and more to my presence and clear the past momentums that have caused all kinds of havoc in your world, you are changing the probabilities. When you do this, I am able to act more profoundly in your world, altering timetables, shifting realities, bringing the highest intention that can be manifest given certain patterns still outplaying.

If you choose to clear all patterns, every block that remains between my will for you and what is now manifesting in your life, than you are making way for me to be more fully in your life, to bless you more abundantly, and to bring you many experiences of a higher quality and finer nature.

Relax. Nothing horrendous, horrible, and nightmarish is in store for you. You are safe in future time where I hold you in my embrace of love. You cannot know what I have planned for you or conceive the wondrousness of it, as you do not know what a beautiful destiny I am creating for you. Realize this truth and be in peace, for I will not allow anything of a dire nature to occur for you. That is why you are being educated as to the times and portents of what is to come through the many prophecies of the day. I bring experts to educate you with the knowledge I want you to have. So you see, I am in charge despite your many patterns.

As you can see, I alert you to patterns when they begin outplaying. The second you catch a whiff of them you can clear them. In that way, we make a great team and there is a lot going for us.

Never fear, miracles are near. If you could see your future as I see it, you would laugh with delight, but then, you might not clear your patterns with such fervor and that definitely is the need of the hour. So keep on and yet, enjoy life more, Beloved. Play, relax and have fun.

Allow yourself to rest. There is no need to stress. Enjoy the magic of your life even while dire prophecies hang and loom near by. They cannot touch you. They are only for you to work on, not dwell on and feel depressed about. For you are safe in the future and your loved ones too. Never fear, for I am the Way to Safety, Serenity, and Ease. I am the Beloved God Presence.

# Trek to the Eternity of the Soul

*Feel the wind beneath your feet*
*as the Heavens lift you into a whole New Life.*
*Feel the Treasured Love that beckons you ever into Freedom.*

*-Babaji*

My Beloved, masterful and skilled is the Soul who leaves behind earthly pursuits and longs only for my presence, knowing all things flow from Spirit. Outwardly seeking that which is translated as peace to the soul can never adequately fulfill the appetite that causes the Soul to ever seek completion.

Insatiable until the end, the Soul longs for fulfillment, wholeness, and truth and yet, so many times seeks this in the world through success, acclaim, and fortune.

Whence did this standard come from causing souls to seek their fortune in the world and having gained it, to sit on citadels of false power looking down upon their fellow man? What pride! What arrogance to assume that treasures won on Earth are lasting and supreme in this universe, of which they are not, for easily they shift and are removed with no warning and thus, the unwary souls build and build again in the Earth Realm, forgetting the deep longing within them to be free in an Eternity of Wondrousness and Peace.

This day you have stepped apart from the world. You have chosen to listen to my voice and in listening, to heed my wisdom and warnings. You have sought a fairer existence than the one that has pronounced it's karmic due the moment you stepped into it.

There is a place that is free from karma, a place of absolute peace and fulfillment. This is an Inner Realm, an inner attainment few gain on Earth. For success on Earth is measured by a quantity of goods rather than Eternal Freedom. Enlightenment, the rarest gift on Earth, touches only those few that dare to make internal journeys towards a greater and lasting good in their lives.

Those who traverse the Inner Realms to find the truth of their being, who long with a deep sense of incompletion the wholeness that awaits them, find what they seek. For that is the Law and yet, how can the Soul find Eternal Peace when it is one pointedly seeking success in the outer world? Where the focus is, where the intention is set, the course begins and that which one seeks is finally fulfilled.

How often have souls returned to Earth, vowing to find the Eternal Truth and yet, succumbing to the status quo, the mark of humanity to claim financial freedom and wealth as the highest degree one can attain, have to return once again. How futile, then, all the riches one would gain, all the earthly treasures that must be left behind when the earthly sojourn is complete.

Then, Soul, where do you stand? What has been all your getting for? What have you accomplished in the eternal sense? What has all the fame, fortune, wealth, and fun ride done for you in an eternity of universes where personal wealth does not measure the soul? The Eternity you must return to with empty hands, with records of uses or misuses, and with nothing else to show but your present state of being.

Thus, the Soul is measured and finds in its incompleteness yet another trek to make, another round to live through all its karmic substance created from beliefs and patterns that keep it ever returning to Earth, ever seeking the way of Eternal Freedom.

When do these endless rounds of rebirth that span millennium cease and the real trek begin, the trek to the Eternity of the Soul in the place of Freedom Within? When is the social climbing enough, the financial rewards no longer alluring, when the Soul seeks its freedom above everything else?

Then and only then has the Soul stepped upon the Path to its freedom. For where the intention is, there lies the course ahead. Then the Heavens bend their heads to view the Courageous One on its lonely trek across a wilderland of past misuses, of beliefs outdated yet binding, of promises to self unfulfilled and unremembered.

Then the clouds open, the darkness begins to lift. Healing and peace begin to enter the life experience and truths, like precious jewels, begin to be the stepping stones to an eternal future that contains within it the freedom to live and be without rebirth, without unconsciousness, without unknowing.

Truth, that Radiant Jewel of Perfection, glimmers it's fragrant presence within the mind, illumines and awakens the Sleeping One, the Inner Presence that for centuries waited patiently to make it's presence known.

In this awakening, True Power is restored, an inner power that propels the Soul into worthy endeavors to fulfill itself and it's Divine Plan, that catapults it into greater and greater life lessons of a Divine intent and that break it loose from the bonds that kept it returning to Earth.

Now Freedom, that ultimate state where Wisdom and Peace crown the Soul in its fulfilled glory, now beckons, now becomes the one great attainment. All of Heaven waits to see if the Soul will claim its Divine Reward, will embrace its Divine Inheritance at last and live free forevermore.

In the gentleness of the day, in the long moments between activity and sleep, ponder well your path, your life, and your choices. For these are binding more than anything can bind. Your will is supreme in your world and by your intentions your future is created. Everything you experience is an outcome of everything you have desired or believed to be your lot in life. Nothing is by chance, for the Universe is created in absolute balance and weighs each life experience to gain the quotient of the next created moment.

Only you can seek and win your freedom. Or, like many souls who remain lost in earthly pursuits, you can return again and again to Earth, never remembering who you are or why you are here, instead following the flock through more getting and accumulating, more having and more doing, forgetting to be your Eternal Self.

It is in your hands what you will shall be. Thus, choose wisely. I Am the Inner Creative Self, the Beloved God Presence Within.

# Claim the Heaven Everywhere Around You

*Heaven is a twinkle in an Angel's Eye.*

-Babaji

My Beloved, Treasures of Heaven are raining their perfection down upon you, gifting you every form of abundance and delight. The skies mirror the beautiful reflection of the Tranquil One, the Buddhic Innocence that rests in the heart of the Enlightened Soul. The still waters mirror the calm of the Transcendent One, who allows only Harmony and Peace to abide in its world. The sweet echoes of songbirds transform the very atmosphere with their heavenly vibration, reflecting the exchanges of heartfelt sharing within Awakened Souls.

How much delight the Divine Ones love to pour forth to humanity in every form. How much abundance greets each soul on Earth each day. Resplendent in its Divine Array of Heavenly Qualities, the Earth is a Queen of Nature, reveling in the experience of unceasing calm. Divine Beings come to visit Earth and dwell in her Splendored Magnificence, understanding she is the fairest of jewels in the Universe, a gift to all her inhabitants.

Such magnificence, such wondrousness is the gift of the Divine One through the Benevolent Earth. The richness all around you in flora and fauna sings in its own unique chords the Love for the Divine Life. Everywhere is the emanation of sound upon your senses, the sound of the Ageless Ones, the Eternal Realities that speak through each and every songbird, ripple upon a pool and wind within the trees.

Yes, Beloved, Elemental Life is here to gift you in its highest form, to bring you back to your senses, the Divine Sense that is your innate Inner Wisdom. Through its highest vibrations, it speaks to your soul of healing, harmony, tranquility, and peace. It is calming, restoring, inspiring, and uplifting. By its very presence, it sings to your soul and brings peace.

Dearest One, do not forget the wealth that is in the Elemental Kingdom, nor the abundant world that is ever around you. For this world, rich with opulence and grace, speaks of the truth of God's Intention for a planet and its people. It is clothed in its finest array, bringing you the majesty and grace of Heavenly Realms that perchance you have forgotten. As if to awaken you from your slumber, it never ceases to pour its good will to you, catching you up into its Divine Majesty and carrying you off into uncharted wonderlands of ever-present joy.

This Divine Aspect of the One through Nature is ever calling to you, ever drawing you out from your busy world into its magical kingdom where it would bestow every joy and fulfillment upon you, blessing you abundantly with its sweet fragrances, colorful birds, tranquil waters, and bountiful breezes. Gently, easily carrying you into ever new joy and wonderment at the astounding audacity of the Divine One to create such perfection in your world and in your amazement, causing you to reflect on where else this Divine Presence is manifest within and around you.

You are cared for so lovingly by Nature Beings who everywhere around you sing songs of joy and thanksgiving. You are cradled in the Earth and gifted all the elements that would nurture you, feed you, restore you, and bring you peace. Everything you would ever need to live in joy surrounds you. It is a silent watchman on the wall of your life, a sweet echo of the Eternal Truth that is yours to claim, if only you would seek it, or perchance, look its way.

Life is so simple. Only humans have made it complex. There is not this complexity in the Nature Kingdom where all creatures live in harmonious Divine Play. This perfection in Nature, the natural stream of things that flows through elements to plant life, to sentient beings, is a thread of Divine Action that clothes all realities with its Infinite Power and Grace, which sustains every level of being on Earth adequately and abundantly.

What a treasure then, is life itself revealed within Nature. What a blessing is your life, gifted to you from on high, with all that you would ever need to fulfill your Divine Plan at your fingertips. What a different world and reality has humanity chosen in remaining ignorant and unconscious as they have utilized these most precious gifts. Without gratitude, they have drained life and left blight where once was Heaven.

It is now in the hands of the Awakening Ones to restore the Earth, by restoring your lives to the Divine Intention, by shifting your Inner Reality to meet the Divine Presence that dwells in perfection within you. To cease to run patterns that cause havoc in the world around you, marring the quiet Sanctuary of Peace known as Earth.

It is time to gift the Earth a precious offering, and this simply by claiming Heaven in one's own life experience. By claiming Heaven, choosing to see the heaven that is here for you and always has been. Then, to live in joy, claiming Heaven fully as it exists all around you, living in gratitude and knowing the happy fulfillment of accepting divinity everywhere it lives, moves, and has its being.

Gratitude and Joy are the keynotes of Heaven. Learn to claim it in your life experience and to bring Heaven into a real and tangible reality in your world.

You are the Master of your Reality. Thus, claim Heaven. Heal all that is not of this Divine Intention for your life and be free. Choose peace and know joy. For these are the ever-present gifts continually waiting for you to receive them. I am the Inner Creative Self, the Divine Presence within you.

# The Violet Flame

*The Fiery Determination of the Soul*
*reaches its mark in the fullest Attainment.*

-Babaji

M y Beloved, tranquility and ease are the qualities of the Buddhic Presence within. These qualities enter ones being as all anger, frustration, and rage are transmuted. The deepest levels of your being, where lie the deep caverns of un-transmuted substance, must be cleared before the Divine Buddha can makes its presence known in the Aspiring Soul. Therefore, it behooves one to clean house, the home of its consciousness, from all that is anti-Buddha within.

Many souls live in this world unaware of the vast regions of anger within their consciousness. Left untouched and unhealed for lifetimes, this great vat of misqualified substance remains to be cleared err the Soul can attain its Eternal Freedom. For, that which is within the consciousness takes up the space that would be the Abode of the Most Holy One, the Sacred Presence Within. Until that space is cleared and there is room, it cannot abide within the Soul. Thus, most souls only experience a tiny dust particle of their divinity, when they could know the fullness of their Divine Self by clearing the space and making room for it in their consciousness.

It is a simple process to heal the un-transmuted substance that has clung to the Soul for centuries. It takes a conscious intention and then, attention on that which has held space in the psyche for it to be transmuted and healed. For the Great Law requires that each and every jot and tittle of misqualified substance be balanced err the Soul is free.

Each piece of the puzzle, each particle of misqualified energy can be placed in the Violet Flame, that most Radiant Flame of Forgiveness, that can transmute all misqualified energy and return it to its original God Design.

For every bit of energy there is a Divine Plan, a Divine Archetype or pattern and yet, through the use of energies in certain formats, they have been encased or clothed in lesser vibrations from the most simplest irritations to the most virulent hatred. Misqualified energy has set its stamp upon the energy field that was used and is now holding a focus of un-transmuted substance.

Elemental Life is then burdened with these substances that once emanated the clarity of Divine Qualities, but which have now become embedded with human qualities, and these are a strain on elementals, causing all kinds of burdens such as polluted water or airs, virulent storms, and the like. Thus, the misqualified energies of the Soul are mirrored in the Nature Kingdom around them and in the many forms that are human creations, through structures, groups, and organizations.

The inner un-transmuted energy not only effects the Soul in its rounds through rebirth, but it effects the environment that it is in and the world that it lives in. Therefore, the collective energies of humankind un-transmuted are creating the pain, suffering, and misery known in many forms in the world today.

The healing of the Earth and the transformation of the planet into an Age of Enlightenment and Peace is directly the responsibility of each soul in embodiment, and the requirement is the healing and transformation of the misqualified energies within them through the Law of Forgiveness, by placing these qualities into the Violet Flame for transmutation.

The Sacred Fire is a powerful action of God that cleanses and purifies energies and returns them to their original Divine Matrix. It is a simple process of alchemy, and a worthy endeavor of each dedicated soul who would do their part in healing the conditions that beset them in the their outer reality and world.

Healing and transforming the inner rage, hatred, anger, sense of injustice, and fear, the Inner Buddha is able to fill the Soul with its presence and radiate its Peace, Harmony, Tranquility, Ease, Joy, and Fulfillment out into the Soul's environment and world. Thus, the Law is fulfilled and each Soul anchors Heaven in its own life experience.

This is a mighty offering to the Earth, a great gift to humanity and must not be overlooked amidst busy schedules and the clamor of the world for attention. For this Sacred Work is such that a world can be transformed in a twinkling of an eye when each soul determines to clean up their own karma, resolve their own issues, and step free into the Eternal Light of their Divine Buddha-hood.

That is the gift awaiting each soul this day. When collectively taken up and applied, the world is transformed. A Golden Age dawns and Peace returns to Earth. I am the Inner Creative Self.

# Awakening to Full Remembrance

*Treasures of the Infinite One*
*pour forth each second of each day,*
*flooding the Soul with the Light Eternal and*
*a Symphony of God Qualities that*
*feed, nourish, and cloth the Budding Buddha.*

-Babaji

My Beloved, the Treasures of Heaven are such that they go unnoticed by the busy world. The Gifts of Spirit are those precious God Qualities that clothe Earth in her finest raiment. For the most exquisite landscape cannot touch the Soul if it is devoid of the gentle thrill that accompanies all of Nature's Wonderlands.

This exquisiteness is the Feeling World of Angels brought forth into physical form through the Nature Kingdom. Nature, with all its beauty, is a step down of Divine Qualities into a physical reality that bathes the Soul in comfort, solace, restfulness, and that uniquely lends its magical healing touch to the areas of the psyche through its exquisite beauty.

This radiant form of God in Action in the physical realm is enough to show the Divine One is ever showering a bounty of gladness, hope, and wondrousness upon its creation. In the eternal sense, all goodness flows forth from the Heavenly Fount of Beingness and pours its Secret Elixir of Life into many forms here below. The most radiant and vibrant is the Nature Kingdom whose Elemental Hosts lend to the beauty, magnificence, and magic as they carefully tend each flora and fauna.

How, then, can humankind not notice with what wondrousness does Life proclaim itself, with what power, majesty and grace, with what outstanding spectacularity and powerful demonstration. This, the power of the Presence of God through Angelic Hosts and Nature Spirits, the Devic Kingdoms, into Nature Herself, and the beautiful and bountiful plant life that nourishes and feeds every soul on Earth.

How came humankind to turn away and join the ranks of other lost souls trumpeting their importance in a world they have created devoid of Nature's Splendor? In their smug reality, where they make themselves Kings and Queens of Materialism, how do they continue on in their dreary existences believing themselves to be Gods, when they have thrown out divinity along with Nature from their lives?

Now is the time to return to the simple pleasures of life, to seek solace and oneness in the heart of the mountain, to find wisdom beside the trickling stream. To grow strong within the forests and to connect with one's Inner Child within the warm oceans.

Now is the time to seek Truth and the True Reality of Being exquisitely displayed before you in the Nature Kingdom, and in joining with the Elemental Beings of Earth, Air, Fire, and Water, to reach up to claim the purest form of divinity in the delightfulness of Childlike Wonder midst the splendored magnificence of God's Perfect Creations.

To sing and dance along a forest pathway, to drink in the pungent smells of pine and cedar, to feel the freedom and freshness of the mountain tops, to soar like eagles above the busy world below.

For where is humanity going with all its getting, and in getting, maintaining? In maintaining, repairing and restoring? Where is the silent exquisiteness that runs through the Nature Kingdom? Where has it eluded the Race of Man, and how can this beautiful Garden of the Divine One be restored?

Freedom is a rare reward to the few who care so much for the Divine Life that all else pales in comparison. The weariness of getting lifetime after lifetime begins to lose the meaning and importance it once had and no longer holds the Soul on its track of endless going round and round, through birth after birth, seeking that which is transitory, useless and unnecessary to the Ascending One.

Now, it is time to see the freedom and truth that is available right before you. To treasure it as the rarest jewel, the greatest reward. To seek its sweet nectar as you enter its Kingdom of Divine Bliss.

Herein lie the treasures that the masses have longed for deep within them and yet lost sight of, believing it was in earthly gains and measures. Here is where the journey of struggle and incompleteness ends and oneness and unity begins, easily and effortlessly displaying its majestic splendors before the Aspiring Soul.

Come, Beloved. Dance with me in the Eternal Journey of Divine Realization. Come live in the fulfillment of the Divine Plan for your life. Come sing the Glories and Hosannas, for the Day is won, the Night is vanquished. Misunderstanding is dissolved and remembrance is awakened into knowledge of who I AM.

The Treasure of Heaven awaits you in the Crowning Glory of your Christhood, in the awakening of your full remembrance and your stepping into your divinity fully.

I am here to greet you at the gate of the Garden of Eden, to beckon you to enter this blessed most sacred place once again. For eons have you toiled outside its perfection, believing hard work and effort would win the day and yet, all it has won you is an endless round of rebirths into a similar life experience where the Garden has remained a dream, lost and somehow forgotten for so long.

Come play with me in the Garden. Drink of its sweetness and know that all its gifts I forever give to you. You need not keep yourself away any longer. There is no reason for you to fight and struggle and have hardship and suffer pain when my Garden Eternal is forever waiting for you to enter at its gate.

Your consciousness is the gate and your attention and intention is what brings you to the Place Prepared, where you can enter the inner state of the Garden of Grace within your being and live Eternally Free.

I am the Inner Creative Self, the Mighty God Presence, beckoning your swift ascent to the Garden where I live and dwell and have my being, Eternally in the Light and Free.

# Today You Can Gift Yourself Heaven

*Heaven is a reality that lives within.*
*Find it there and it shall emanate from your being*
*like a mighty Light in the darkness.*
*From this inner vantage point,*
*life takes on a new meaning.*
*Purpose guides your Destiny on Earth,*
*and everyone around you is transformed.*

*-Babaji*

Beloved of My Heart, the challenging times ahead need not cause fear and trembling, for they are but appearances upon the Screen of Life that are yet to come, though not absolute. Divine Will and Divine Intention forever holds a different outcome before humanity, and it is for each one to grasp this intention and choose to live out of its reality, which is the keynote of this time.

As each soul claims the Divine Life, aligning their will and intention with the Divine Plan for their life, many inner changes will occur very swiftly and very dramatically within each one, bringing the Divine Blueprint into physical manifestation.

This is a time of sober reflection, a time of going deep within in a quest for understanding all that is happening now on Earth. For the rumbling and roaring of the tide of karmic recompense is upon the world and many are being caught in its clenches and are finding themselves immersed in the Great Travail.

This long overdue condition is a result of many choices made collectively by the humanity that inhabits this planet. Not one incident is a result of some foreign interference. Rather, each soul can look within and find the causes and cores of the condition of this world there.

This, then, is the simplicity of the task before us, because each soul can then cast its vote. Will it choose to perpetuate duality and the pain and suffering that has been an outcome of the war between dark and light, or will it choose oneness, the Eternal Oneness that is its soul's Divine Birthright and the inheritance that is waiting for it moment by moment as it makes its life choices?

Then, in choosing Heaven, Oneness, the Divine Life and the Divine Way, your soul comes into harmony with the Divine Plan. In aligning with this highest intention for your life, a Divine Destiny is born and that which is your greatest gift can flow forth to a world in travail and begin its restoration, healing, conveying peace on the deepest levels of being.

Can you imagine the power of a humanity deciding in this moment of Earth's history to cease war within themselves? To stop suffering and perpetuating duality, schisms, separateness, and aloneness? To instead choose Heaven in their own life experience, claiming that as a reality in their consciousness, being, and world, establishing a harmonious way of life through loving interactions with others? Can you imagine the power of each soul healing the shadowed aspects within that have lent to the dramatic undoing of the world? Can you see the power that is now in humanity's hands to stop the Great Travail and instead implement a Golden Age?

These are powerful times, blessed times and each soul is called forward to make their mark in the Book of Life what they choose for the future of life on Earth. Each vote counts and will make its presence felt in the times ahead. For, as each soul chooses to live, whether in perpetuating darkness or claiming harmony and peace, this shall make a difference to the Earth. Once each vote is in, there is a grand tallying, and then it will be known whether the future of life on Earth will be a continuing of the plagues, wars, and cataclysmic events of an unbalanced eco-system or a Heaven Experience filled with creative endeavors lending to the Restoration Earth Project.

What will it be, O, Soul? What will you choose? How will your life be? Choose wisely! Be conscious, awake, and aware through this time ahead, and heal quickly the schisms within your own psyche, for each schism, each pattern and limiting belief has its counterpart in an Earth condition that all are now facing collectively.

Heal the conditions of Earth within you and very last appearance of darkness in your Shadowed Self. Through forgiveness, release yourself from lifetimes of dramas and traumas with no end. Heal the scarring and core beliefs that have decreed you to a way of life that is about suffering and step forward free to live in an Eternity of Oneness, happiness, joy, and peace, which is your Divine Inheritance, which is the Divine Blueprint for your Soul, which yearns and calls and longs for its fulfillment within you, and which you have for so long held back through your beliefs.

Now is a great time on Earth. Now is the time to rise up and claim your freedom at last, to say no to suffering en mass and to heal the causes and cores of suffering in the world. A time to come apart with your families and communities of light to create a different reality, a life where harmony, happiness, and peace rules, because within you this has been firmly established and thus, the outer reality comes to mirror the inner state of your union and oneness with the Divine Self who you are.

Thus, Heaven reigns in your world. It permeates your life experience and it sings its glory out into the ethers of the world and transforms the Dark Night into a Glorious Day that dawns a Golden Age of Enlightenment and Peace as has never been seen on Earth.

Today is the first day of the Life Glorious. Today is your opportunity to heal the inner voices that have caused torment and pain in your world and to choose instead Harmony and Peace. Today it is imperative you cease your sleep and slumbering and face the world condition with open eyes and a deep understanding that you are witnessing the repercussions of the collective choices of each person on Earth.

Today you can step away from the miscreation and choose a world that sings with the Divine Harmonies it was intended to outplay. Today you can gift yourself Heaven. I am the Inner Creative Self.

# Inner Service

*Treasure hunting is the greatest Joy to the Soul*
*who knows the greatest treasures lie within.*

*-Babaji*

It is a Glorious Day, Beloved. I enfold your heart in a luminescent gold that you might feel the Divine Power you are emanating in your being as you carry on through the Inner Service you so spectacularly render not only to yourself, but to this planetary home each time you pray and invoke the light, each time you go deep within to clear a pattern.

Such blessed events are spectacular alignments with Cosmic Planetary Beings, who in seeing the need for a major shift in the control of the world and the powers that be, find the healing must first come within the Lightbearers of Earth. Then, the circle of oneness reverberates through the many and a mighty healing is wrought. As the inner alignment occurs through the healing of patterns that have kept souls enslaved and locked into systems that no longer serve, an outer victory is won.

How precious then, is your Service to Life. How joy filled and wondrous the victory. How sweet the feeling, to know the greatest gift has been offered to Earth this day and that a major clearing has taken place, bringing a greater light to America and the world.

So it continues, the Sacred Service many have now entered into these last days, the last days of servitude and slavery on any level. You can have hope. You can look to the rainbow in the sky and see the promise that all will be well. As you understand the patterns and choose to heal them, you will step free from every last condition that has bound you.

Every sorrow and grief will slip away and with it, unhappiness and pain, every last bit of hardship, struggle and suffering, until you enter my abode completely and know Divine Peace at last and a world that is transformed, because your world is transformed and your perspective has changed.

Thus, you experience life on a whole new level with a breath of Divine Reality and Truth, which is far more edifying and entertaining than the shadowed concepts of what is happening here on Earth.

There are wondrous happenings each moment of each day, victories upon victories on deep inner levels for each and every soul. There is a new sense of freedom ringing in the hearts of humanity, and where does it come from but within the gentle radiance of the Divine Hosts that serve this planet night and day.

O, Beloved, if you could see the victory before my eyes, you would be in peace forevermore, for you would know what a great service your Inner Work has been. Now, carefully, we change the wording into your Inner Service, which it rightly is, and move away altogether from concepts of work and working hard, which is a momentum of the past and no longer needed in your present reality.

For the truth is, it is all Divine Play, a magnificent play of energies, healing, and extraordinary transformations. Each day, each moment gifts each soul an opportunity for a great healing, a tremendous release and relief from pressures within and without, from conditions that have kept them bound and gagged with no where to turn and no way out.

There is a way out of these planetary conditions. It is an inner way to align with me, anchor to Divine Truths and hold to Divine Realities that sweep away old conditions as if they were dust upon the floor, making room for the bright shining victories there for each one.

You, my Beloved One, must reach up to the stars and behold your Divine Radiance there. You must see the Divine Perfection who you are and hold your vision upon that star of your own self birthing, born right into this physical reality, which is your heart, mind, soul, and physical body.

Watch as your physical conditions continue to shift as the inner alignments occur. Watch as victory upon victory marks your trek across this earthly soil and how appearances, dark, ugly, and fierce, are swallowed up in the Mighty Victory, which I Am.

The Heavenly Hosts are singing praises of victory through you this day and in truth, a great victory is won, not only in your own life and consciousness, but also in this humanity. Think not that this is a light shift, for this is major and it shall set the stage for many victorious actions to follow as you move into full power.

Keep on, for the way is ever clear before you. Each challenge is but the opening of an opportunity for great healing and change. Without these inner shifts, the outer conditions cannot budge. Look then to the Inner Service, to the inner facilitation of healing and the shedding of the Shadowed Aspects now are ready to be realigned with the Divine Intention. Watch, O, Blessed One, for your life changes completely now. I am the Inner Creative Self, the Mighty God Presence

# The Only True Reality is the God State

*All Great Souls who have made their trek across the earthly waters*
*have earned the right to claim their Full Dominion in the Earth,*
*take command of all aspects of their worlds,*
*and cease to live in duality.*

*-Babaji*

The Glorious Light abounds. My Presence is with you. You, my Dearest One, have once again set the mark on the goal of our union and this Divine Promise awaits you in its fullness. For having set aside all other goals and intentions, having lifted them up into my hands or cast them into the Lake of Sacred Fire, you have shown me your willingness to abide by my will alone and no other.

In so doing this one thing, you have shown your faithfulness and your commitment to our union as the absolute reward you would seek in this world, and I gift it to you. For that which you seek you shall find. So has been the folly of many lifetimes of willful wandering in earthly circumstances, drawing to the self all kinds of experiences out of the longing for the greatest, deepest fulfillment, which comes from our oneness. Misplaced and misunderstood, you have sought to find me in the outer world, to gain power, prominence, wealth, stature, assurance, and stability in things temporal and transitory.

Now you have seen and understood how your soul has longed for our reunion and oneness, which has been the underlying motive beneath all earthly longings and their subsequent manifestations in your world.

How I love and adore you. How I love to embrace your precious heart tenderly and shed all worries and fears, all over-concern with earthly events, whispering to you instead of the calming action of my presence with you. Still waters, calm seas, tranquil skies, these are the qualities of the Divine Realm in which I live. All else that brings concern and upset to your soul is neither of my sphere nor of my experience. In aligning with me, entering the oneness of our union, you step into this New World and New Life and bask in the tranquility and ease, which I know, live, and have my being in.

Then, the Rest of Ages transforms the weariness of your soul in its countless earthly treks and wipes away the stains, the hardness, coldness, and pain of that arduous journey, replacing these conditions with Peace, Oneness, Happiness, Joy, and the ever-present lovingness that pours ceaselessly from my heart.

Now, in this glorious day, our union is greater, our oneness more complete, and ever it shall be in the days to come as you surrender all to the Glorious Light which I am, to the Eternal Presence within you, the Indwelling Spirit of the Most High, which you are in the center most heart of your being.

Innately pure and perfect, your journey into duality has cast many shadows upon your path and yet, now through many lifetimes of experience, your appreciation of the Eternal Truths are greater. Having experienced their antithesis, you now hold precious the God Qualities that once were taken for granted and which were not known as the great treasures they were because there was nothing to compare them to.

Now you stretch your wings and fly to freedom. Now you cease to traverse dark, unknown roads and instead, call for my Light Eternal to guide your way. Now is Life Everlasting begun in its newest most jeweled form, in its precious splendored delight, for peace I grant you this day and wealth beyond measure, wealth to fulfill all things, to complete the vows of this embodiment, and to enter the Divine Life that is Eternal.

All this I grant you. All gifts I bestow. All righteousness (right use) of God's energies I give you. As you have aligned with my will, so you are Divine Will in action in your world. Your consciousness I fill with my Great Presence of Love and Compassion for a world. Now experience me in your every day and in your every meeting. Allow me to radiate my goodness, lovingness, and caring to everyone you meet.

Allow me to show you the compassionate understanding of every life situation within and without, and guide you unfailing upon the path of the right use of your God given energies, until you are completely anchored and stabilized within the Divine Presence which I am and which you are.

Now, for a moment, allow me to touch your third eye and quicken the awakening of your memories of your divinity, of long moments past when your life was fully divine and nothing else was in your reality.

Allow me to bring you the remembrance of your True Identity apart from any identity you have claimed in this world, for these things are transitory, and as you pass from the screens of life you shall not take the honors of earthly life with you, nor the wealth or possessions. You will instead understand the greatest value gained was your Christhood, your Buddha-hood, your Eternal Oneness with my Presence, and this rare Jewel of Attainment is the only lasting thing this world could offer you. All else is left behind.

Remember this in days to come, as you seek solace in the outer world or fulfill projects, for these can never give the glory to your soul your full alignment with me can give. These are only vehicles of learning and growth, opportunities for right use of God's energies and to balance old records. Other than that, no glory here on Earth can equal the glory of your God Presence in the Heavens. Therefore, choose wisely. Understand the True Path and design your life so you can receive the greatest assistance on this trek to Divine Oneness.

I love, cherish, and adore you, Beloved. Know I am ever with you in the days ahead when the world spins and turns, creating ever new realities. Remember the only True Reality is the God State and claim that as your Crown of Victory over any earthly endeavors. I am the Inner Creative Self, the Mighty God Presence.

# The Masterful Way to Take Dominion of Your Life

*The genius of the Ever-present One is unfathomable to the
conscious mind for it transcends basic learned knowledge and ideas,
allowing a vaster range of information to be disseminated.
Wondrous is the response in life when this Genius Within
is accessed and applied, for then the trek of the Soul becomes
a masterful journey on the Path to Enlightenment.*

*-Babaji*

Beloved of My Heart, the Winds of Change are now upon you
as planetary systems shift making way for the New Era. So many swift
changes are about to occur within your own life. You will be astounded
by the direction I carry you in. For, unbeknownst to your conscious
practical mind, there is a Divine Plan unfolding, allowing me to benefit
you in the greatest possible way with my insight and fortitude.

The doorway to the future opens before you, a magic entrance
into a whole new life and way of being. Anchored spiritually, your trek
is more about personal unfoldment as you shift the last patterns of the
Shadowed Self, coming under my full dominion completely and absolutely. It is then your life no longer looks the same. Planetary shifts and
astrological configurations no longer have their influence on you in the
way they may have before this inner alignment with my will.

Thus, the cycles roll and many find themselves entrapped in conditions that are little more than their own inner limitations finding an
outer expression. Because you choose to clear these away and stand free,
my magnificence, great heart, power, and attunement with Spirit will
prevail. All uncertainty will be dissolved as you enter the Grand Cross
of your final passage into my abode and heart, the Heart of Eternity.

Understand then, your astrological cycles depend upon your willingness to overcome the Shadow and step into freedom configuration upon configuration. Because you are willing and able to do the inner work that sets you free in each circumstance, you gain the greatest growth and learning from each life experience.

This catapults you into greater awakening and advancement on the Path, and is a masterful way of taking dominion of your life. All blessings can flow to you during times where others feel the greatest terror in the undoing of their lives, while you, my Beloved, Initiate of the Light, use each circumstance as a stepping stone to your Eternal Victory in the Light. Yes, it is a glorious passage and I am setting you up in a place of comfort and ease where you will know my profound love for you and my ability to work with the cycles and mitigate the impact in your world.

Now see the astrology of this coming year take on new meaning as you realize the opportunity ahead to enter this Grand Cross as a final point of release of the Shadow into the Light, stepping forward into a whole new way and system, for the Way of the Shadow no longer works. It affords you no great victory or promise, nor does it enhance your life in any way. For you have ceased the need to learn through hardship, struggle, upset, and travail.

Instead, you have moved into a Glorious Life, the Life Victorious, where you meet each challenge as a Masterful One, healing all schisms you find within, for you understand the mirror of the outer world. Thus, your passage is safeguarded. Soon you will understand the perfection of the plan and will look back at the times of uncertainty with a greater understanding and knowing of how much I love you and how much I am able to assist you, provide for you, care for you, and make all situations right.

On this happy note, I say, your future life is a glorious example of a Masterful Being and there is nothing less that will manifest. For I have measured your heart's intention with the inner fire of your soul and the dedication of your mind and seen your Victory in the Light is secure.

Keep on and win the Night. Make your safe passage to the Land of Eternal Bliss and Oneness. There you will find me, forever uplifting you to ever-new heights of Divine Perfection and Wonder. This is only the beginning and truly, you haven't seen anything yet. I Am the Inner Creative Self, the Mighty God Presence.

# I Continually Perpetuate Your Lifestream

*Radiant and wondrous is this Path of Light.*
*Beyond the specters of earthly existence, the Real Self pours*
*forth its Divine Radiance into the souls of humanity and holds the*
*framework for each life experience. Unseen and many times unnoticed,*
*this Silent Presence keeps the watch that the Soul might find*
*the real treasures fulfilled at last in Eternity.*

*-Babaji*

**M**y Beloved, wondrous is each new day and the sparkling opportunities to live fully in my presence. To sing the songs of joy and fulfillment, to bask in the splendor of my magnificence, to embrace me fully in every moment and know I am ever with you, guiding you safely to the greatest fulfillment you have ever known. My one purpose and intention is to bring you to the safe shore of my Eternal Abode and in drawing you back home, give richness, magic, and wonder to the trek you are now walking.

I am always showering my love and light upon you. Each moment of each day I pour this forth unfailingly and hold for you as you make your journey through life. Whatever choices, whatever direction you choose by your own free will, I am here, loving, supporting, and cherishing you. No matter how far you enmesh yourself in earthly affairs or in the shadowed aspects of self, I continually perpetuate your lifestream with my Divine Essence, with the Breath of Life, which is my Eternal Gift to you.

My Joy is great this day as I see your determination to return to our oneness and know me absolutely as the Divine Part of you, which I am. I tremble with the sweet fragrance of our imminent union and await the Heralding Angels in their announcement of your completion of the rounds of rebirth and your candidacy for the Ascension.

Light, radiant light, streams forth this day, enveloping you in its presence as I hold the Immaculate Concept for you and remain faithful and true in my support of you. Each moment of each day I hold this unfailing love for you and gift you life, pure life. With that stream of life, you choose moment by moment how you will utilize it and if it will be a beneficent energy for the world or a harmful one.

You can qualify my energy with any quality you choose and in placing the stamp of your conscious will upon it, the energy flows forth and does either damage or good. Once it completes its circle, returning into your world the same energy qualification you sent forth to life, you experience that which you put out. In that way, you learn about the right use of energies and how harmful energies bring destructivity into your world, while beneficent energies uplift and bless you.

There is this ever constant flow of energy taking place through you and therefore to be wise, understanding the wise use of energies, is essential to the trek back to oneness and wholeness. Through this infinite expression of Divine Energy you learn the lessons of life and you see the results of your personal qualification of energy. This is the precious gift of my presence, to continually provide you with pure unadulterated Life Energy to use as you will and learn by this use, gaining mastery and skill in handling energies.

I bless you this day with the powerful Presence of Love. May this LOVE be sent out through you to all life, assisting a planet to embrace the Divine Qualities, which I am. As you choose to be a vessel of this pure Love and Light, so shall your energies be constantly qualified with your divinity and the returning energies be so blessed and momentous, you will be constantly experiencing a Symphony of Divine Qualities pouring into your consciousness, being, and world.

I love and bless you with my Wisdom and Radiant Light. May each day forward be one of mastery and attainment displayed in the purity of Life Energies flowing forth to humanity. I am the Inner Creative Self, the Mighty God Presence.

# Open Your Life To My Ever Present Wisdom

*Restoration of the Divine Faculties is the process whereby the Soul takes on Immortality, Oneness, and Truth. In the beginning, this divinity was known and experienced. Over time, the Soul descended into a conscious awareness of duality and began playing out dramas under that code. Once satiated to its fullest, the Soul understands the full gamut of earthly life and the realities that come from the play in duality. Complete with these processes, the Soul seeks freedom from rebirth, freedom from the rounds of karmic outplay, and freedom to live in its divine state once more. It is then the Heralding Angels record the Soul's one pointed intention to return to the heavenly awareness it once knew and lived in. Ministering angels assist as the Soul makes its trek out of illusion and pain back to the Life Eternal.*

*Once the Abode of Peace is gained, once the last footsteps on the journey home are complete, the Ascension is won and the Soul transcends this earthly realm to reunite with its Divine Presence in Heavenly Kingdoms in the consciousness of peace that passeth all understanding. It is then the Soul is a God Free Being once again, the rounds of rebirth and all karmic cycles complete. The True Life begins, a momentous life that is lived in absolute serenity, knowingness, and awake-ness forevermore. This is the state of True Freedom and reward of all souls who seek the Eternal Oneness they once knew in the beginning.*

*-Babaji*

O, My Beloved, how beautiful is the treasured experience of our loving and the consciousness you have entered where you see me, converse with me, know me, and learn all that I am here to teach you.

Accepting me as your true Guru, the true teacher, you open your life to my ever-present wisdom beyond the earthly awareness many great teachers on Earth hold in their consciousness. Therefore, Truth, unadulterated and pure, is what you receive from me. For I dwell in Eternity, in the Eternal Realms where there is no duality, no limited thought forms, no illusionary beliefs to hold one back.

I see and live and have my being in the eternity that knows only Truth and Oneness with the Divine Source, which has only perfection in its consciousness, being, and world. This wondrous state I enjoy and have always known. It is what I draw your soul back to and what I have come to teach you as the Way, the Truth, and the Life.

Dearest One, how blessed is your trek when clothed in my understanding, lit up by my wisdom, straightforward because of my truth. How blessed is this journey when you walk it with me hand in hand, knowing I will never lead you astray, knowing I will take you on the shortest path, the quickest path to the ultimate goal which is Eternal Life.

When you are one pointed, placing this goal first, there are no other lines of force created to take you on this path or that. Instead, your focus is steady, your intention secure. We walk swiftly to the goal, uninfluenced by the world around you and what others are doing, for you have found the way to put Eternity before all else even while you allow me to pour my blessings through you to humanity.

Thus, your life's gifts become an effortless outpouring of my Immaculate Heart to a world while you the Soul, holding the intention for our union in Eternal Oneness, stay focused and aligned with my will for you, which is freedom and peace. You take the steps laid out before you one by one, each with a secure foundation I provide for you. You see our union as the one great goal and no other goals come in your consciousness to cloud the journey. You understand you need have no other goals but to live aligned with my will, continually setting your course for our union and oneness, while all other things are given to you effortlessly as I give you your breath.

Therefore, you come under my dominion. You seek me in my absolute form and align your will with mine and I take care of the rest. I guide you into right circumstances for your greatest growth and awakening. I bring you into your Inner Wisdom and Wise Knowing step by step. I bless life in the balancing of your karmic records and begin clearing these swiftly through my Service to Life. For I am the one now living through you, accomplishing all things, setting my world aright, clearing my karmic past, and stepping into Eternal Freedom through you. Therefore, it is done easily, effortlessly, swiftly, as I know the shortest route, the easiest way, and the simplicity of the process.

No longer is there human groping for understanding and the way to go, for I am the All Knowing One. I am the Eternal Light within you. I see and know all and therefore, can never be confused, lost, or alarmed. Rather, I live in complete awareness, completely qualified and astute in all affairs of the world and the intricate details of your life. I see the way to go and I lead you easily and effortlessly.

As you pay homage to me, no longer seeking my wisdom in the outer world through others who may have yet a few clouds in their judgment and a few beliefs untrue, I can guide you absolutely. For, I know the way. I am the Way. I am the Truth. I am the Light. You need not seek any further.

For I am the greatest teacher you will ever know, the greatest guru you could ever find. I can be a tangible presence in your life, if you will but call to me, align with me, seek to know me, and bring me before you face to face. Then you will see my magic unfolding and the unraveling of the mystery of your life processes, as you gain the greatest meaning and growth from each life passage.

I await you in my Abode of Peace. Seek me and you shall find me. Know me and you will know your self in your truest form. Relinquish the hold the world has upon you. For what have you gained lifetime after lifetime but learnings and growth through hard circumstances, through unfulfillment and loss. What have you gained, but was lost once you passed from this life? What stayed with you after the journey, but the limiting beliefs gathered and the lack of freedom to live in Eternity, because your will chose other avenues of enjoyment and fulfillment apart from God's Plan?

You chose to seek that which could have been found within your Divine Self and lived out of for eternity. You drew to yourself experience after experience that caused you to ever change your opinions, and therefore cloth you with ever new beliefs that continued to hold you in the rounds of rebirth, keeping you from the Eternal Freedom which is your birthright.

What good has it been? Of what importance is the success of this world, a transitory thing that comes and goes and leaves the soul empty at the end? What is fame, but the passing of the world spotlight upon you for a time, but not for eternity? What is wealth, but the gaining of financial stability in a world that is unstable and which can alter and shift at any moment?

With all this getting, what have you gotten once you pass from the screen of life and find yourself back in the Inner Realms? Where are you now from all this worldly gain when this world is transitory, a place of learning and growth and not of Eternity? How can you think to build up treasures in such a world, lifetime after lifetime, when it is lost again the moment you pass on?

What then is the point of continuing to seek success, fame, and wealth here? That is my question for you today, to reflect on, ponder, and come to terms with. What has been the value in all your earthly getting, of claiming status and success from other souls who have been just as lost as you in the world? When is it enough? When is it not worth it any more? When do you come to your Divine Senses and realize true building is to build in Eternity your Divine Presence, which I am and which I am ever here to bring into your consciousness, being, and world.

O, Beloved, how grateful I am you have come to understand these things, to leave the world and all its getting and accumulating behind, seek our oneness absolutely and leave the rest to me. For I shall provide for you abundantly, clothe you in my Perfection, Harmony, and Grace and gift you a fulfilling life in the midst of your trek to our oneness. I will pay back the karma you have accumulated through Divine Service through your soul, my vessel. I will right all wrongs, heal all schisms within your psyche, and set your world aright, easily, effortlessly, and abundantly.

I am here for you in the deepest recesses of your being, showering my light through your life experience and calling you ever home to our oneness. It shall be, for you will it and so do I. Together, united and one in purpose at last. The magic has just begun.

I love and treasure you, my Beloved. So sacred, precious, and beautiful you are to me. Gift me the one treasure only you can gift me and that is your full allegiance to my will, to my Immaculate Heart, which loves you so absolutely and which gifts you your very life. I am the Inner Creative Self.

# Destiny Speaks at the Dawn of Your New Life

*Blessings abound as the Christmas Angels gather to*
*sing Hossannahs to the new born Lord of Light within.*
*This day, the Christic Fire is born within you as the Christbearer,*
*the Lord of the Heavenly Light within. This Flame fanned into a*
*Divine Presence is the Holy Christ Self of each one.*
*Ever present, it resides in the hearts of humanity, clothing their*
*life experience in the Christic Vision of the Awakening Ascending One.*
*So it was for Jesus, who claimed this Divine Self as his own,*
*and so it is for every man, woman, and child on this planet.*
*Who will come to adore him this night?*
*Who will come to treasure the blessedness*
*of this Christic Presence within?*
*Who will align their lives completely with this Sacred One,*
*which is the True Nature and Beingness of every Soul.,*
*the True Light, True Way, and True State,*
*ever waiting to be embraced.*

*-Babaji*

Cherish this day, Beloved, as the Angels sing Hosannas of Divine Grace, for Mercy has descended from the Heavens and is clothing the Children of Light with its Heavenly Raiment. Yes, this is a day of glory in the highest, in praise to the One Eternal Light within you.

This day you can step free from the fetters and chains that have held you back. This powerful moment in time and space is destiny unfolding before your eyes. For Destiny speaks. It is the resounding voice of the Divine Presence within you, the Christic Light that has ever guided your way through your earthly experience, which has ever whispered Divine Truths in your inner ears and called you to nobler acts and higher attainment.

Now the Light descends and is most glorious, enfolding you in golden, white, and rose. The Angels sing so near to you. Listen within the stillness of a quiet moment and hear their sweet songs, for they come to announce a Great Awakening and advancement, if you will, into a whole new era, way and beingness being birthed within you as I speak on this earthly plane, into the earthly consciousness, filling you and enfolding you in radiant, glorious Light.

This is your Christmas Gift, poured out to you from Holy Angels. This gift is a most cherished offering. I treasure its portent for your life, for now you pass through the portals where there is no turning back, no descent back into earthly ways of unconscious actions and behaviors. Now you awaken more fully and stand in the Earth an Awakened One, anchored in the truth of my presence, seeing life in its clearest, most absolute form.

Thus, your world is transformed, your life is changed, and that which you thought might be and hoped would be is even swept away before the glorious gift of my Eternal Presence with you, lifting you up into a life heretofore unfathomable and unseen. This is the glory of my presence with you and my gift is the gift of Heaven's Treasures, the full awakening and advancement of your soul in the Ascension.

Be at peace this day and know the nurturing Light of my Presence descends into the very depths of your psyche and removes the stains of sin and the consciousness of sin on the deepest levels of being, for you need never undergo the challenges spawned from these misdirected beliefs about yourself again.

You are a Divine Being and I claim your victory this day. The Light descends, the Treasures of Heaven pour forth, and the Healing Angels administer to you, deep within your psyche. Where you have held destructive thought forms within the folds of your garment of consciousness, now they are removed.

Now Light descends and transforms the darkness that was there, the dark thoughts and dark feelings held so sacred and yet, so unreal all these lifetimes. They are dissolved because you choose it so, because you align with my will and thus, I bring glad tidings and Hosannas. Holy Angels appear and minister to you. The Christ within you is born and is raised into its full manhood, wedded with your soul in Holy Union.

Now it is time to cease your crying and moaning, your unhappiness and sorrows, your catastrophes and limitations. It is time to shed these outworn garments and step into the Radiant Light that I Am. It is time to raise your sights to behold the blessed Angels with you and to see and know the truth of who you are.

I call you into Full Awakening and Full Knowing. As you have called for the truth, so it is given unto you and with it, Peace Everlasting. Now you shall know who you are and from whence you have come, and all the glories you have experienced in your life histories and all the attainment, mastery, and skill you have won. You shall cherish this moment and this Christmastide, for I beckon your soul to full recovery in the Light, to the full advancement of your Heavenly Splendor, which is your divine clothing to wear for eternity.

You are a Blessed One. Wait and see the glories before you as this deep healing is completed and you move into this next era of your life. Watch the victories won so easily, the blessed days that move in procession one after another as you enter the New Life I have waited so long to gift you. Now you are ready to receive it for you have received me with all your heart, mind, and soul. Thus, my gifts of many treasures now enter your life, swiftly, easily, effortlessly, and your life is transformed.

This is the glorious year you have awaited. Mark it well in your mind. This is the Life Victorious you have aspired to. Understand its import and impact on your life experience. Through this Christmastide, much Light, Healing, Grace, and Illumination will be pouring forth to you in preparation for the Dawn of this New Life on January 1st.

Sing with me the Divine Praises to the One Eternal Love that lives ever-present at the heart of your life, energies, mind, and soul, for we are one and in our oneness a Mighty Work is done. Now it is complete. The Light is transferred, the healing complete. Now, watch the magic of the days ahead and the glories and gifts that pour from my heart to yours. I am the Inner Creative Self.

# A Grand Awakening is Taking Place on Earth

*Hearts ringing with Joy in silent expectation,*
*hold fast while the Christ Within appears.*
*It is in these Sacred Days of Christmastide when*
*humanity as a whole can bow their heads and know the*
*Everlasting Promise of the Christic Flame within their hearts.*

*-Babaji*

My Dearest One, the precious light of the Solstice has descended and the Eternal Light within you has emerged, as if out of the darkness is born a Great Light. Like a flower's seed planted in the dark and moist ground, it grows ever upward seeking the light until it arrives, and in its arrival, finds beauty, magic, and wondrousness.

For in the Light, it is greeted with the loving embrace of the Divine One in Nature, enfolding it in the warmth of sun and replenishing and revitalizing it with the dew and rain. What perfection awaits the simplest flower as it ascends to the Light. Can you think it is any less for you?

The grandest Awakening of Hearts worldwide is taking place now through this Christmastide, as souls throughout this Blessed Earth stop their busy lives to contemplate the deeper meaning of Christmas. Embracing the concepts of the Love of God in their lives, they come into greater humility and lovingness and begin giving to their fellow beings gifts of love and caring, gifts that say they have entered the Magic of Christmastide.

In the Heavens, there is rejoicing as many Angels draw near to watch the hearts expand within the once busy humanity. At last, a moment of contemplation and stillness. At last, the childlike wonder and laughter. At last, kindness and lovingness. At last, the desire to gift others and let them know they are loved.

It is a precious time, a sacred time, and this Christmastide is most special for there is an awakening on this planet that is significant at this time, an all encompassing quickening revealing to those that have sought enlightenment the truth of who they are. In knowing this truth, they step forward to share their Light at a time of vast changes on the planet.

It is time to know yourself in your absolute true form. It is time for you to reach up to the star of your God Presence and claim that one with all your heart, with all your mind, and with all your soul, choosing to live in that Sacred Reality forevermore. It is time to be all that you can be and in this gift to humanity, the Light of the Presence can bless, heal, and transform the world around you and teach you the Way of the Quiet Buddha, who comes with a silent tread to bless all life that he/she encounters.

O, blessed Light, what a magnificent display of souls turning heavenward, desiring to be pure, whole, entering the oneness at last. Blessed are the Angels, witnessing from the Heavens such a beautiful, victorious sight. For as these ones seek, so shall they find and as they set their intentions clearly, so they shall know the Oneness and live in the wholeness of their Divine Selves at last.

This is a precious time, a momentous period on Earth. Enter the preciousness of the hour and know my love is with you this day and always, uplifting, inspiring, and ascending you into ever new heights of Divine Awareness. I am the Inner Creative Self.

# God's Glory in Nature

*Rainbows of Brilliant Light descend upon the Earth,*
*flooding it with Healing Light as Holy Angels on each Ray*
*pour forth their Essences of Love, Peace, Tranquility, Ease, Joy,*
*Fulfillment, Compassion, Wisdom, Power, and Truth.*
*Those who align their consciousness with this Great Outpouring of Light*
*are filled and sealed in the power of the Eternal Presence within them.*

*-Babaji*

O, Brilliant Day, O, Glorious Light! How I spread my Wings of Light to embrace the Ever-present Wisdom, which thou art. How I love to dance in the golden sunshine, play among the turquoise waters and drink in the deep emerald green of the forest.

I stand upon the mountain of God Attainment and beckon you to my side, so you can see the glory of which I am ever beholding, even here on Earth. For you have sought to understand a world in turmoil and find your way midst suffering and disease. You have glanced heavenward from time to time to gain meaning from it all. Now, in this glorious moment, I call you to my side. Be here with me. Abide with me and look out from this lofty height of God Awareness, God Understanding, and God Compassion and tell me what you see.

Do you see the beauty and magnificence of God's Glory on Earth called Nature? Can you pour your mind's essence into the heart of the Nature Kingdom and hear its silent message of Healing and Peace, of Renewal and Strength, of Understanding and Wisdom? Can you now see the perfection of the plan that gave Nature Wonderlands to the striving souls on Earth and which caused a beautiful planet to be created for enjoyment and peace?

How healing is the nature beauty all around you, how restoring. How rewarding to journey into the midst of this Nature Kingdom and become lost midst its splendor and glory, and become lost to a world that has taken up too much of your time and energy, which never ceases to rush around you in its tumult, winding on and on to the next circumstance, the latest challenge.

There is a Nature Wonderland ever near you calling silently to your soul, "*Come my Beloved and join me in my Nature World, for I will restore you. I will enfold you in my healing arms of Compassion and Mercy. I will tame the wildness of your mental state and bring you swiftly into tranquility and ease. I will polish your Divine Nature so it shines in your view so you can catch a glimpse of your True Reality. I will shed my Light upon your Pathway and bring you into Peace.*"

How gracious and bountiful is this Nature Kingdom with all its Nature Spirits who frolic and play in joy. How beauteous is this tranquil world created to gift you surcease and rest, and this such a gracious gift from one who has ever been misjudged and maligned as being the cause of harm and hardship in this world.

In truth, humanity has altered a world created in pristine beauty by its thoughts, actions, and feelings. Through many diverse beliefs, the world has been reformed, recreated if you will, through atoms and electrons rearranged to create after belief systems of a collective unconscious within the minds of humanity. What you have believed you have created, and now the Earth has moved so far apart from the Heaven World it was created as with its beauty and splendor.

At last you have embraced the possibilities of the healing of a world and the transformation of the Earth back to its original and perfect state. Many of you now embodied on Earth, carry this Flame of Truth within your hearts and your message is of Hope and Peace.

Through this sacred time ahead, the opportunities will be many to gift the Earth with qualities of Divine Awakening, Divine Inspiration, and Divine Attainment. For as you claim these in your own life experience, many will be inspired to do the same and thus, a wave of light coming from those who dwell on Earth can be met by a wave of Absolute Joy and Peace from the Heavenly Host and together move this planet into an era of Enlightenment and Truth.

How Glorious a time to be alive. How precious each heart that lifts itself up to be the truth of its Divine Self, and through that Awakening, gifts a planet with such Love and Light to forever change its state. This is the Sacred Promise of this time and therefore, I share with you the import of the blessed Nature Kingdom in its ability to restore, renew,

and revitalize you at every turn, as you make your way into the Ever
-present Joy where I dwell. I am the Inner Creative Self, the Mighty God
Presence, ever watching over your soul and guiding you safely home.

# The Golden Light of Peace

*Remember your tryst with the Eternal Spirit Within*
*first and foremost each day.*

-Babaji

Beloved of my Heart, how the Winds of Change, howling around you and yet, you are enveloped in the warmth of my Divine Radiance, which pours its Golden Light of Peace into your field and keeps you safe from all disturbance and harm.

How the calamities line up for the Earth, parading before your earthly view and yet, strong and unmoved you remain sealed in my Light, which is invincible and eternal and therefore, not subject to earthly changes or planetary strife.

How I adore you, my Blessed One, you who look to me so constantly for guidance in this time where there is soon to be a complete undoing of a world you have loved and known. And yes, your innermost thoughts and feelings on this subject are resonating with the truth of what you have been shown and given at inner levels. Therefore, remain true to that which you have seen and know despite the lack of awareness that surrounds you.

You are being shown this reality because you do not need to dwell in it. So many glories await you, a Life Victorious in the midst of calamities and unrest. You have done your work. You have been diligent in facing momentums and moving yourself out of harm's way within and therefore without. I would say, keep on, for this is the area of greatest opportunity for you. Through the Inner Work, you have the ability to set yourself completely free in the Light of God that never fails.

So many blessings are now to come upon you. Such abundance as you have not yet known and why not, when I am extremely wealthy and able to provide abundantly for you? Why not, despite the intentions of others and the unraveling of their lives, because they have held rigidly to patterns that must come undone err they can be healed?

Look not around you, but keep focused with my Inner Light. For, in this way, I will guide you safely to your next level of awareness, easy graceful steps into greater and greater fulfillment of your Life Dreams and Divine Plan, and all this so swiftly, so effortlessly, that you shall be amazed at the simplicity in which you shall change and be in your New Life, happy, carefree, and living in ease. No hardship, hard work, trauma, or drama, just a relaxed excited move into a whole New Life and therefore, way of being.

I bring you into joy, greater and greater joy as I pour forth my full abundance into your world and this crystallizes in your life. I shall advance you into greater service that will feel like greater play, with greater freedom to be in all those places you have longed to be. Now, my gifts expand and we enjoy together Heaven on Earth.

Be at peace and stay awake. The time comes soon. I am here and very active in your life, preparing the way to your final victory. I am the Inner Creative Self.

# Know the Abundance of My Heart's Intention

*Treasures of Heaven's Grace descend and envelope the
Light Bearers of Earth, while the lands tremble and roar
through the cataclysmic events ahead.
The Light is the Mystery of this time enfolding those
Faithful and True in the midst of earth change.*

*-Babaji*

Prayer and meditation is the keynote of this week as we move to the New Year and beyond into the Light Eternal of each new day. Blessings descend, Beloved, and with it the wealth I have longed to gift you. Treasures of Heaven are the gifts of my heart, the longing of my soul to gift you everything. To fill your days with blessed events, bring health, vitality, warmth to your life experience, peace, freedom, love and a sense of being carefree, alive, happy, and well. How I long to bring you every gift and have you know the abundance of my heart's intention for you.

Each time you clear a pattern, you remove the karmic circumstances, which bound you in a very different life than what I have chosen for you. Your karma keeps you ever immersed in dramas and hardships that are not my intention. Rather, the outplaying of certain beliefs gathered through experiences have kept perpetuating the darkness that has surrounded you lifetime after lifetime. If you think of a world free of pain, suffering, hardship, lack, a world abundant and free, glimmering with the wealth of my God Presence, radiating love and joy into every heart and peace reigning supreme through every land, this is what I will for you and all life. Everything not of this beauty, majesty, and peace is not my intention.

This then, is the key I give you. For when you see conditions and life experiences around you not reflecting this higher keynote, you can understand you are experiencing the outcome of a karmic accumulation through beliefs you have carried in the subconscious, which are now taking mental, emotional, or physical form.

Understanding this equation brings the Path to Enlightenment into greater simplicity as you work your Sacred Alchemy to undo the patterns and miscreations that have long strangled out the beauty and light from your being. Weighed down by unnecessary hardship or lack, you have striven to create beauty and magnificence in a world limited by your Inner Reality, handicapped from your full expression and the full power that is my self within you.

Healing these schisms in your psyche is an important keynote and focus. As each pattern is healed, my presence is able to pour its gifts to you. Abundance begins to replace lack and limitation. Harmony and Love replace hardship and unkindness. Prosperity and Joy replace financial stress and frustration. All conditions that are imperfect and bring hardship to you are merely the past creations wanting to be set free, wanting healing and transformation. These can be transformed easily, setting you free to live a whole New Life in a whole new way of being that is abundant, beautiful, and fulfilled.

You can step forth and experience life fully, live fully, and know freedom on every level. This is my New Year's gift to you, the understanding of the Path to Freedom through healing every condition that is not and never has been My Will for you. Through the Sacred Fire, through advanced techniques like TheQuest, through the ancient art of Ho'oponopono, you are able to clear yourself of these life histories and engulfing patterns and know freedom, peace, harmony, and joy once again in your life experience.

What a wondrous knowledge, to know you need not go out into the world to struggle for these things, or try and make them happen against all odds but rather, turn within and heal the conditions there. For each condition healed will then allow my Presence to be more fully active within you and my gifts expanded into your life experience.

So simple and yet, so profound to know I hold all things for you. Clear the way to my treasure trove. Set a clear intention now to face every pattern and use the tools before you to heal every last condition that is less than my perfection. As you do this, know you are accepting Heaven into your life experience. You are making room for it and bringing it fully into your consciousness, being, and world. As you anchor Heaven, you send a resounding reverberation around the world and the vibration of Earth is raised another notch. All beings can breath easier, freer, because you accept the God Presence where you are and all the miracles that come with my destiny within you.

Know my treasures await you and my heart pounds with expectation of your reception of all my gifts. Ever I stand, waiting at the door of your consciousness, ready to flood forth my Majesty and Grace upon all life through you, in you, and in every life experience, saturating you with the blessedness of my Divine Presence and the Divine Life.

Sacred Living is now. Claim it and move this world into a new era of Enlightenment and Peace. Let the Earth no longer cry in its Great Travail, but free it by freeing yourself. Cease the inner warring and cataclysms and watch how the Earth begins to mirror your inner tranquility, peace, beauty and perfection.

Cease playing out the dramas not befitting a Divine Being and live as the Divine One you are, who I Am within you. Claim me as your True Reality and let the illusions of the past wash away by the truth of my presence with you.

Let me be your Guiding Light, the Beacon of Hope that carries you across the sea of your un-transmuted self to the shore of your Divine Reality. Light Eternal awaits to claim you fully, to hold you in its safety and peace, to swallow up the darkness in which you once dwelled. Take heed. Follow my keys to your mastery, attainment, and Ascension in the Light, for I am the Lighthouse of Truth beckoning you to my safe shore as you traverse the Dark Night in the Sea of Unreality. I am the Inner Creative Self.

# Seek That Which is Eternal and Everlasting

*A New Day has dawned and with it the Glorious Sun has risen.*
*A New Day is born and with it the Glorious Light enfolds all.*
*Each morning the Majestic Presence of the Divine One*
*pours forth its Grace upon the world, as the Sun rises into view,*
*pouring its Glorious Light upon humanity.*
*Each day the people of this Earth can know anew the profound love*
*of the God Presence through this Sacred Ritual in Nature.*
*Each day we are reminded the Light is Ever Present, Eternal, and Alive,*
*continually pouring its Healing Light into the world.*

*-Babaji*

O, Blessed One, my heart is full as I bring you close to me and enfold you in my love. How often you have turned to me in past days and sought my guidance, assistance, and help. How often you look to me for knowledge, wisdom, and the way in which to travel life's pathways. I am ever here to guide you for I see the way. I am the way of your Eternal Life.

Dearest Heart, how I have pondered the best way to convey, through these letters, the majesty and grace, which is my Divine Birthright and yours. How I have rejoiced as you have taken my words to heart and lifted up your mind unto things eternal. How grateful I am you seek that which is Eternal to complete the earthly rounds of rebirth, acknowledging this completion and fulfillment of your trek into unreality, duality, and all that was there for you to learn.

You have likened this trek to a virtual reality experience and your Shadow Self as the vehicle you step into to explore the world of duality, the consequences of this duality, and its perpetuation in the consciousness of humanity. I agree. This vehicle has afforded you a wondrous journey into the dark and unknown world of the Shadow, where unreality and separateness is an experience the Soul can drink deep of with no judgment or blame, traverse the wonderland of human creation, experiment with energies and see how they return to the one sent, go deep into the depths of human emotions and become seemingly lost in an experience of anger and hatred, even while I enfold them with my Love Eternal and hold fast for them, sustaining their life and being that they might explore, and in their exploration, learn all.

All this, that the Soul might learn quickly by experiencing repercussions of misuses of energy, what happens when one dwells in duality, how the Shadow Self can seem so all engulfing to the mind, blocking out the Sun of my Divine Reality, leading the Soul ever wandering on pathways of darkness, seeking the Light and yet, many times not knowing the way to free themselves from the patterns and momentums of their shadow side.

This is a wondrous experiment of learning so you can gather a wealth of knowledge of good and evil with my blessing and with the Love of God pouring continually upon you, ever-present though unseen and unknown by the mind immersed in a dark world, ever there to lift the soul back up out of the experience of duality into the Eternal Light, showing the way as a lamppost on a dark pathway to the Life Eternal.

Now you have known this journey through the dark realm of human understanding and experience is complete for you. Your Soul rises above the plane of duality seeking that which is eternal and everlasting and I am here, awaiting your journey back to the realm of safety and peace in which I dwell.

Far from the pain of this planetary home, in deep inner realms where Enlightened Beings dwell, I have my Abode of Peace. I live and move and have my being in the Realms Eternal and I sing songs of praise and thanksgiving every day, knowing the blessedness of a life lived fully and absolutely in Divine Awareness. I have many Friends of Light who have spoken to you, guided you, and who seek to assist your soul upon the Pathway of Light that you may enter True Freedom as they have done and dwell in this freedom forevermore.

The Glorious Sun symbolizes my presence with you. Forever I am here, even when the Dark Night enfolds your consciousness and you cannot see me, I am pouring my light upon your world and blessing you with my many gifts.

Nature is a wondrous reflection of the Divine Life and of your journey back into the Oneness. Seek the solace, rest, and respite the Nature Kingdom will afford you in the days to come. Let this New Year and new time be a joyous communing with the Nature Kingdom, for you will increase in health and well being from this experience.

As you hold to my presence, receiving me daily and listening to messages I lovingly bring to you, know I am working at deep inner levels with your soul, assisting you to free yourself from those bonds that have no reality in the Higher Realms where I dwell, have no purpose and therefore must be shed and released err you are free to return.

Stepping into Eternity is simple. It is a moment to moment process of releasing the hold the Shadowed Self has on you by choosing to dwell in qualities of the God Self, like harmony, love and joy. When your consciousness moves from this Place of Peace into the shadowed realm of upset, disturbance, anger, or hate, move quickly to heal the part of you crying for attention, who wants a voice in your world and is clamoring for you to notice and embrace it, that it may be healed and restored to the Divine Image.

Now use the many advanced and ancient techniques to heal this part of self, this Shadowed Aspect, restoring it back to the Light Eternal. In healing it, you heal the histories and karma that surrounds it along with the events that took place in your past. In healing the past, you free up the present and remove the harmful circumstances yet to be created in your future. Therefore, past, present, and future are cleansed by this specific healing at the appropriate time, each aspect rising up into your conscious awareness at the perfect time for its healing.

As a Soul of Great Mastery, you afford yourself this opportunity of great healing and the cleansing of your karma each time an aspect arises and you move into discomfort.

The way is won, simply, easily, and sometimes effortlessly, as you learn how to work with these inner aspects, embrace the Shadow, and heal and transform them for the last time. As each aspect returns to the higher vibration and intention, it experiences an ascension and thus, day-by-day you ascend. Each aspect ascended is another part of you that dipped into unreality and duality that has been restored to the Divine Intention, the Divine Knowledge, and Divine Awareness.

As you do this work, your wisdom increases as your Innate Wisdom is restored. The part of you that had limited ideas and painful experiences is healed and raised. It now dwells in a higher awareness, emanating the qualities of its divinity through you like love, truth, and hope.

As you walk this Healing Pathway, you are moved into greater and greater peace, tranquility, and ease. You become the Wisdom of the True Self. Each time misconceptions of the Shadowed Self appear, they are cleared, healed, and transformed and you step into compassionate understanding, unconditional loving, and truth.

Moment by moment, you choose to live out of my Divine Reality, healing everything that rises up in your pathway contrary to my Eternal Presence and thereby take command of your life, setting your course for your Eternal Freedom, stepping free from all that has bound you to a different reality than that which I Am.

Now I have shared with you the great wisdom of how to extricate yourself from the shadowed awareness that has ruled your life in this experiment with duality and how to step free in each moment to be who you truly are and live in the Eternal Freedom which I am.

This simple process of Inner Alchemy will bring you safely to the shore of my Eternal Life, which is my gift to you and my will and intention for you. As you choose to return to Eternity, understand there have been many things created in your journey through the duality experience and these must be resolved, healed, and transformed, for the Creative Energy, which I am, is continually pouring through you, activating all you will and intend, creating that which you have imposed upon your consciousness.

Therefore, every belief you hold whether it resides in Truth or not is an active will in motion. As my Creative Energies pour forth into you each day, these beliefs are activated into real life situations and conditions. That is why this experience has been so engulfing to the point where sometimes you feel constrained and confined by life events. The source of these troubles is within your subconscious where you are holding beliefs contrary to the Eternal Laws of my Being and are creating a very different reality than what I am willing and intending.

It is in your best interest to pay attention to this subconscious body and bring the necessary healing salve to wounds there, for this is a powerful part of you, a creative aspect that must be free in order to create after the divine images I hold for you.

Wherever there is lack, uncertainty, hardship, sickness, or pain, understand this is the miscreation of your subconscious beliefs calling to be healed and that must be transformed err you can live in the perfection I hold for you.

This is the most misunderstood, yet powerful body, wreaking havoc over and over again in the lives of humanity. Even still, many have thought God is the one that has poured out his wrath upon a world, caused all these disturbances and is continually punishing souls for deviating from His Will. This is a false belief that puts responsibility somewhere else for life's challenges when in truth, each soul is creating his or her reality and each is responsible for it.

It is time to come awake, be aware, and heal the miscreations and misuses of the Divine Energy that has created sickness and death in a world made up of atoms and electrons that are eternal.

In Eternity were you born and thus must you return, once you have had your fill of duality and all the repercussions and hardships that come from a life lived contrary to Divine Principles and Divine Truth. Now you can return without judgment and blame, for you are loved and treasured. Now you can fully understand, your journey into the Dark Night of your own miscreation has afforded you much wisdom and growth.

Now it is time to reclaim your Divine Heritage, return to the Light of your God Presence, live Eternally Free, and heal the energies collectively wreaking havoc in the world, which are tearing it apart through cataclysmic activities as we speak. All these things born out of the misconceptions about life are ready to be healed as we step into the Grand Intention for this New Millennium on Earth.

I love, treasure, and honor you, Beloved. Know and understand the depth of my compassion and care for you. It is time for your return. I hold open my arms to embrace you as you pass through the last portal of unreality to my Abode. I am the Inner Creative Self.

So concludes
Part One of the Letters from the Inner Self.
I hope they have blessed and enriched your life as they have mine.
Editing them brought me to the next level in my soul evolution,
facilitating a powerful metamorphoses and equally
profound experience as when the letters
were first delivered to me in 1998 and 1999.
This has shown me the powerful inner and outer changes
that can take place no matter what level a person is at and
how the letters can continue to be a source of great
wisdom and advancement no matter how far one has progressed,
or how many times you take this journey with the Inner Self.
Such is the MAGIC of these
Letters from the Inner Creative Self.

With Much Aloha and Many Blessings,
Aurora Juliana Ariel, PhD

# Part Three

# Appendum

# About The Author

Whether its pioneering work in the psyche, bringing out her landmark discoveries in global conferences, writing books, leading TheQuest Trainings, or expressing her musical talents, Aurora Juliana Ariel possesses the proverbial Midas touch. Her brand of alchemy is the sacred sort, yielding a gold one can only discover within. Pioneering doctor and scientist, author and musician, entrepreneur and producer, mystic and healer, Aurora is a Renaissance woman for the New Millennium.

A Humanitarian Futurist with an extraordinary heart and offering for humanity, Aurora Juliana Ariel, PhD has dedicated her life to creating a better world through three vehicles focused on positive planetary change: the Earth Vision Foundation (Lemuria Rising - Earth Vision Center Project), Institute of Advanced Healing (bringing out TheQuest worldwide) and AEOS (a new frontier in multimedia arts in healing, inspired music, books and films).

Creator of TheQuest (a breakthrough psychological healing system), #1 Bestselling Author, and Award Winning Author of the Earth 2012 Series, she is a Pioneering Doctor and Healer whose research and work have given her a profound understanding of the psyche and the tools to heal an ailing humanity. Working with countless individuals with miraculous results, she has made many landmark discoveries bringing a new understanding to our present planetary equation. She speaks eloquently of the significance of this time in Earth history and the challenges before us, bringing a timely remedy and insights inspiring people worldwide to make a difference. She holds over 35 certificates and degrees in advanced healing methods as well as a B.A., M.A., and PhD in Psychology. She is also a Kahuna, the successor of Hawaiian Kahuna, Shaolin Grandmaster Pang.

All of this pales, however, in comparison with the work Dr. Ariel has done on herself and her work directly in the psyche with countless clients over many years, resulting in the development of her Counseling Theory and Healing Practice, TheQuest, which she calls the 'Ferrari Model' of Inner Healing work.

A Spiritual Scientist in the Laboratory of the Soul, Dr. Ariel took her vast body of knowledge and went deeper on her own quest for healing. She discovered a way out of pain and suffering, a transformative technique that changed her life and brought tremendous healing to her clients.

Dr. Ariel has taken TheQuest to the next level and offers it as a complete Self Healing System that includes her powerful seven step Self Counseling Technique. Her reason for bringing it to the people, rather than simply releasing it to professional counselors is simple. She wants to bring healing to a world in desperate need.

Dedicated to positive planetary change, Dr. Ariel sees this period on Earth as a time when we, as a humanity, desperately need to uncover and heal the subconscious patterns she believes is at the heart of the dire conditions we are presently facing. When we accomplish this, we become the peaceful, loving, happy individuals we were meant to be and the world changes around us.

For more information about Dr. Ariel, her work and products see: http://www.AuroraJulianaAriel.com. To support her efforts, you can make a tax deductible donation to the Institute of Advanced Healing at: http://www..IOAH.org. Your donation can also donate *TheQuest: Heal Your Life, Change Your Destiny* books or Complete Self Healing System (book, Healing Journal, CD) to rehab centers, prisons, hospitals, health retreats, safe houses for the abused, addiction, abuse, and youth at risk programs, or place of your choice. *Your donations are greatly appreciated!*

# TheQuest

TheQuest is a revolutionary breakthrough Counseling Theory and Healing Practice that includes a complete Self Healing System developed by Dr. Ariel after years of extensive research and work. It is designed to bring timely knowledge and a missing piece to rehab centers, prison reform, addiction, youth at risk, 12 step and other programs, greatly increasing their success rate.

For practitioners, it is a way to move your clients quickly from upset to peace, and to help them quickly resolve deep issues, step free of limiting and self sabotaging patterns, addictions, and dysfunctional personality traits, and realize their greater potential.

For the layperson, it is a way to gain greater understanding and mastery of your psychology, empowering authentic self-expression, and creative fulfillment.

For couples, it is an essential ingredient in conscious relationship, where each person works with their own psychology as issues arise. Greater harmony and clear communication can exist when the focus is on resolution through loving, compassionate interactions.

## The Institute of Advanced Healing

In 2000, Aurora Juliana Ariel, PhD founded the Institute of Advanced Healing, a non profit organization in Hawaii, to bring forth her life's work, TheQuest, which includes TheQuest Trainings, Classes, Counseling Sessions, Support Groups, advanced healing products and services.

Dr. Ariel developed certificate-training programs and set up a model chapter in Aspen, Colorado in 2005 to be duplicated around the world by graduates of TheQuest Master Counselor and Spiritual Leadership Training Course.

She has successfully worked with youth at risk, addicts, abusers, and the abused, people with serious illnesses and trauma, and a host of dysfunctional personality traits and life conditions with tremendous results.

She has given classes to teens at High Schools, released TheQuest to the public on her websites, TV, radio, support groups, and via her

Ask Dr. Aurora Column, and is now training people in her seven level Certificate Training Courses provided through the Institute. For more information see http://www.IOAH.org and http://www.TheQuest.us.

## The Human Dilemma

The work at the Institute of Advanced Healing has a very clear focus. To bring TheQuest to a world in dire need. The subconscious programming that has created the human condition with its propensity for misery and suffering must be healed. People worldwide need to understand their psychology and learn how to become masters of their destiny, rather than victims to their fate. The cause of suffering must be healed for the world to begin to reflect the noble ideals that are encoded in the hearts of humanity.

When people are engulfed and entrapped in their human patterns, a higher destiny is never fulfilled. Instead, the destiny that plays out is from this programming. The degree that the higher nature, which Dr. Ariel calls the 'Authentic Self,' can express through the individual, the more the person will be able to experience a higher awareness and ability to attain a greater mastery over their life circumstances. Presently, this is very rare on Earth. Even in the spiritual communities of the world where the greatest trainings and highest information is attained, there is a continual dysfunctional aspect to people's lives, because the subconscious patterns are not being addressed. They are being suppressed or spiritually bypassed, while they continue to work their havoc.

It has long been believed that people cannot change their personality traits or heal their addictions. The best that can be done is for individuals to understand their patterns and strive to overcome them. But this method does not work because physiologically the limbic system, the part of the brain that is activated under stress in what has been called the Fight and Flight Syndrome, is different from the area of the brain where the will and determination is found, which is in the frontal lobe. Therefore, under stress, the individual will revert to Fight and Flight, and the subconscious pattern will begin running. They will move into survival and seek substances or run other addictive behaviors to alleviate suffering. Physiologically, the blood will recede from the frontal lobe impairing will and therefore control.

When the deeper patterns have not been addressed and healed, people will understand their addictions and strive to stay sober or substance free, but if they undergo a series of life stresses, it will be easy for them to fall off the wagon. This is because the subconscious has been left out of the equation.

Currently, because the deeper work is not being done, there is only an 8% success rate in rehab centers and addiction programs. The programs today help strengthen the individual's resolve, but do not provide a complete healing. TheQuest Seven Step Counseling Technique provides the 'missing piece,' which can greatly increase the success rate at these centers and with people suffering from addictions of every kind.

## A Breakthrough Technology

Understanding the human dilemma and being concerned that psychologists today normally only scratch the surface when working with clients, thereby keeping people coming for sessions for years without any real movement, Dr. Ariel developed a way to move people quickly through their issues, and heal their underlying patterns. Her revolutionary method provides a complete resolution, healing, and breakthrough in each session.

If you would like to sponsor or support Dr. Ariel's work and the Institute's mission to bring TheQuest to communities throughout the world, donations are tax deductible and greatly appreciated. To make a donation, please go to http://www.AuroraJulianaAriel.com, http://www.IOAH.org, or http://www.TheQuest.us

## TheQuest Life Mastery Path

When you understand your psychology, you have greater control over your life circumstances. As you master TheQuest tools and learn how to heal every condition from within, you have a greater command of your destiny. Your Authentic Self is given room for a fuller creative expression in and through you and a new passion and excitement about life returns. You wake up looking forward to each new day and what amazing things will happen next. Unexpected events and synchronistic meetings increase resulting in key alliances with like-minded people for a greater purpose. Life takes on a sweeter quality, as you know you are fulfilling a sacred destiny. TheQuest Life Mastery Path training is available in TheQuest courses, providing you with the tools and knowledge of how to free yourself from every pattern and condition that has limited you, kept you feeling disempowered, burdened, or held back, so that you can realize your full potential.

## Heal Your Life, Change Your Destiny

When you heal your life, you change your destiny. It is as if you are defying a powerful law like gravity. For the human patterns within you are creating a different reality than the Life your True Nature would give you. Clearing the way for this Authentic Self to lend its wisdom and power to your life, allows you to fulfill a higher destiny.

## TheQuest Counseling Sessions

While Dr. Ariel is largely on sabbatical focusing on writing, appearances, and training individuals worldwide, she is from time to time available for personal sessions and for shorter personalized training programs. These are weekly or bi-monthly sessions over 6 months to 1 year that include Life Coaching and Counseling sessions along with personal training in TheQuest Life Mastery Path. Dr. Ariel is also available at times for personal 7 - 14 day retreats, where her focus is completely on you and your optimum health and well-being, and for Total Life Intensives where every area of your life is addressed and transformed.

## TheQuest Training

Dr. Ariel holds TheQuest Certification Training Courses all over the world. If you'd like to sponsor her in your area, receive counseling sessions or life coaching, or receive certification as a Life Coach and Counselor, please email her at: info@aeos.ws.

TheQuest Training consists of three level certificate courses. Levels 4 - 7 are for those who want a career as a Life Coach, Counselor or Spiritual Leader in the Organization.

# Become a Certified Life Coach and Counselor

TheQuest Life Coach and Counselor Certification Course provides an in-depth study of psychology in a format that is experiential, life changing, and empowering. These highly informative trainings, within a compassionate caring environment, can be taken via phone from anywhere in the world.

Each course is unique per the student and their current life challenges and is therefore, a journey to the heart of these conditions where they are completely healed and transformed, returning you to Authentic Self awareness. You master tools to heal self sabotaging patterns, addictions, personality traits, and dysfunctions, deal effectively with health and career issues, and transform challenging relationship dynamics. In this way, you transform and empower your life while learning how to help others.

As you learn how to clear a pathway to the Authentic Self and its inner wisdom, you begin to give it more power in your daily life and to fulfill your higher Destiny Potential. By mastering your 'shadow,' you learn to live in the Miracle Consciousness. This is when you begin living a Miraculous Life.

TheQuest Life Coach and Counselor Training is a one-year (or accelerated 9 month) certification course working directly with Dr. Ariel each week. Highly experiential in its application, this program gives you the life mastery skills, knowledge, and tools to become a Master Life Coach and/or Counselor, with the ability to practice anywhere in the world. Doctors, Psychologists, Health Practitioners, Life Coaches, and Ministers may qualify for the accelerated training program with Dr. Ariel for TheQuest Counselor Certification.

# TheQuest Programs

## Healing Lives, Changing Destinies

Total Life Transformation Program

Life Coach & Counselor Certification Course

Counselor Certification Course

Miracle Weight Loss Program

Relationship Healing

Addiction Release Program

Women's Empowerment Program

After Rehab – Maui 21 Day Retreat

Maui Rejuvenation 21 Day Retreat

In-depth information on all programs and products
can be found on the following websites:

http://www.IOAH.org
http://www..TheQuest.us
http://www.AuroraJulianaAriel.com

# A New Frontier in Multimedia Arts

Media is one of the most powerful ways we can facilitate change today because of its immediate affect upon the psyche. Understanding this, Alchemists of the New Millennium know that transmitting positive images, ideas, and language of a beneficial and healing nature can quickly shift consciousness, open up new doorways of thought, and empower individuals to be their best selves.

Through conscious media, we have a tremendous opportunity to assist in this next evolutionary leap in human consciousness and safeguard against the repetition of the mistakes of the past, assisting humanity to become conscious stewards of the earth and inspiring them to bring forth their greatest gifts and achievements on behalf of a people and a planet. By helping catalyze this quantum shift, we become Alchemists of Media who have an important role to play in this New Millennium.

At AEOS, we are determined to make a difference! All our products are exquisitely designed with the highest quality materials, highest vibration of colors, images, and subject matter, and transmit, energetically and creatively, the highest frequencies. We believe our vast array of extraordinary products and services are destined to transform millions of lives throughout the planet.

AEOS, Inc. is a Multimedia Production Company founded by Chairwoman and CEO, Aurora Juliana Ariel, PhD. TheQuest is a proprietary revolutionary breakthrough technology she developed, representing one of the Company's five collections of inspired music, books, and films, placing AEOS on the leading edge in the new psychology/self help genre.

Look for more exciting AEOS products soon, as well as Dr. Ariel's upcoming books in the Earth 2012 series, which delve further into her insights on the worldwide awakening and global renaissance she believes are birthing a New World. To order our products please go to our website at: http://www.AEOS.ws

# Healing Inspired Music & Media

Dr. Ariel has studied the powerful influence music and media have on the psyche. She believes "transformational media is a key to creating the quantum leap in consciousness so necessary at this time, if we are going to avert the many dire potentials before us and positively affect the evolutionary cycle of our planet." Understanding that conscious media can have a profound and healing influence upon individuals and even transform lives, her greatest love has been to translate her knowledge into multimedia productions that have a healing, uplifting, and inspiring effect. In 2003, she founded AEOS, Inc. to bring forth her inspired music, books, and films. In her words, "My joy is in translating the knowledge I have gained into transformational multimedia productions that facilitate positive change within the psyche of humanity, profoundly affecting the consciousness of the planet and assisting humanity to advance forward into an Age of Enlightenment and Peace."

## Books & Music CDs by Aurora

### Earth 2012: The Ultimate Quest - Vol 1
*How To Find Peace In a World of Chaos*

### Earth 2012: Time of the Awakening Soul - Vol 2
*How Millions of People are Changing Our Future*

### Earth 2012: The Violet Age - Vol 3
*A Return to Eden, The Regenesis That is Birthing a New World*

### TheQuest: Heal Your Life, Change Your Destiny
*A Breakthrough Self Healing System*

### Letters From the Inner Self: The Indwelling Spirit
*An Illumined Pathway to Freedom, Enlightenment, and Peace*

### Renaissance of Grace
*Aurora's World Music CD with Bruce BecVar*

### Gypsy Soul, Heart of Passion
*Gypsy World Music CD by Bruce BecVar & Aurora*

### River of Gold
*New Age Music CD by Bruce BecVar & Aurora*

# Earth 2012: The Ultimate Quest
## How To Find Peace in a World of Chaos

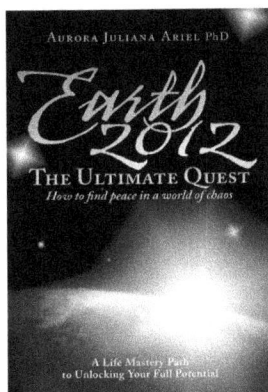

*Award Winning 1st Book in the Earth 2012 Series*
By Aurora Juliana Ariel, PhD

Cataloging the profound shift presently taking place within the psyche of humanity, Dr. Ariel points to the fact that we are living in unprecedented times! Weaving a blend of sacred prophecies, prophetic visions, and scientific predictions around 2012, she unveils a glorious potential that is casting its first rays of light on earth, illuminating the Dark Night we are presently passing through, and providing a "missing piece" to traversing the challenges of this time.

In this first book in the Earth 2012 series, Dr. Ariel guides the reader on a personal quest, providing 7 Master Keys to Inner Peace and a revolutionary breakthrough Self Counseling Technology, TheQuest, that is easy to apply. Distilled into seven powerful steps, this healing process is designed to accelerate a personal and planetary transformation that could help end suffering on Earth.

Her message, "If we want to avert the dire potentials before us, we must look within and unlock the subconscious patterns behind our challenging life conditions."

*For timely updates, sign up at http://www.AuroraJulianaAriel.com*
*More books in the Earth 2012 series are coming soon!*

# Earth 2012: Time of the Awakening Soul
## How Millions of People Are Changing Our Future

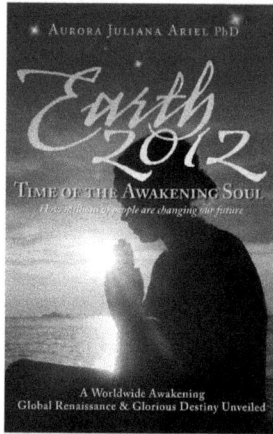

*A Worldwide Awakening,*
*Global Renaissance & Glorious Future Unveiled*

### By Aurora Juliana Ariel, PhD

The Earth 2012 Saga continues with a Journey into the Miraculous as millions of Awakening Souls alter the course of Earth's Destiny. Weaving a prophetic vision of an Illumined Future, stories of extraordinary encounters reveal the significant time we are in. Find out if you are an Awakening Soul. Take the 22 Master Qualities test.

*This inspiring, prophetic book speaks to a Soul Awakening that if embraced, can take humanity through a quantum leap into a future Eden that has forever lived as a vision within the hearts of humanity.* —**John Gray, Author of Men Are From Mars, Women Are From Venus**

*This book rises to the heights of poetry, unveiling a majesty of human potential like a torch in the morning light. It adds its brilliance to what is silently arising all around us.* —**Jonathan Kolber, Circle of Light**

# Earth 2012: The Violet Age
## A Return to Eden

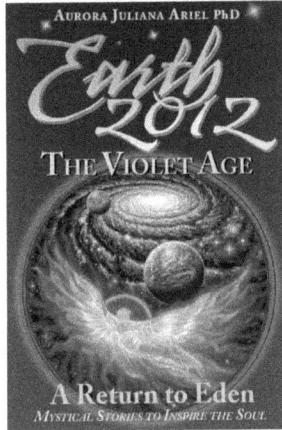

## By Aurora Juliana Ariel, PhD

Miracles abound as the Earth 2012 saga continues. A host of phenomenon behind the Great Awakening are impacting millions of people worldwide. From extraordinary encounters to mystical experiences of every kind, a quantum shift is taking place in the consciousness of humanity.

This book takes us further into the mystical side of our present planetary equation and unveils the mystery behind the Violet People and the unique destiny that drives them to turn the tide at the 11th hour, saving humanity from untold disasters.

While darkness increases on the planet and humanity stands facing gaping jaws of disaster on a Grand Scale, a glorious New World is being birthed from within the psyche of humanity.

*"A clarion call to consciousness awakening to itself, the Earth 2012 series quickens spiritual unfolding by lovingly guiding you through one of the most difficult and transformative periods in human history."* — **Leonard Laskow, M.D., author of Healing With Love**

# Earth 2012: Oracles of the Sea
## The Human Dolphin Connection

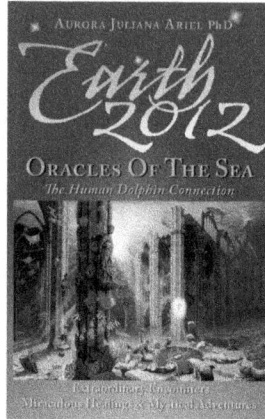

### By Aurora Juliana Ariel, PhD

For the past 33 years, dolphin interactions with humans have increased dramatically, resulting in a host of miraculous stories that include extraordinary encounters, mystical experiences, profound visions, telepathic communications, unexpected healings, life changes, inner transformations, and spiritual awakenings. Amazingly, these experiences are similar to events recorded at the advent of the Golden Age in Greece.

This worldwide phenomenon speaks to a critical time in Earth's history, as awakened from normal lives, diverse backgrounds, and belief systems, the thousands of individuals experiencing these encounters share a common bond and responsibility. Weaving the threads of this phenomenon from its most ancient historical significance into the present, we find we are moving into a future that may yet be our most Glorious Age.

*"The Earth 2012 series will speak to hearts around the world. It will quicken the Awakening in many who have tried to make sense of similar experiences. It will bring relief to those who have pictured a negative future. It will help others realize the potential that is being birthed within us all in this extraordinary time. After working closely with Dr. Ariel on this project, I am excited to see the powerful ramifications it'll have on people around The world."* — Jack Canfield, co-author of the Chicken Soup for the Soul series

# Letters from the Inner Self

## *The Indwelling Spirit*
### *An Illumined Pathway to Freedom, Enlightenment and Peace*

This inspiring, timely book opens the door to a Soul Awakening that if embraced, can create a joyful life filled with Love, Harmony and Beauty. *--John Gray, Author of Men Are From Mars, Women Are From Venus*

Spend some time each day with these beautiful writings and feel your life rise on wings of love. *--Gay Hendricks, Author of Conscious Living, Co-author with Kathlyn Hendricks of Conscious Loving*

This is information that nourishes the soul. *--Wayne Dyer, Author of over thirty books including The Power of Intention.*

The resounding echo through this book is that we are loved. Through this LOVE of the Indwelling Spirit we are inspired to see, know, and love ourselves in the way that God loves us. When we love ourselves absolutely, we give ourselves our best life. Embracing ourselves from this Divine Perspective, we live Sacred and Abundant Lives accessing the Great Power Within.

As we consecrate the moments of our existence to a Higher Purpose, we allow the Divine Plan for our life to fulfill itself in and through us. Living in the Miracle Consciousness, we enter the Miraculous Life, a sacred and richly fulfilling existence where we uncover Life's Sacred Mysteries, witnessing to the majesty and glory of our Authentic Self as we walk our Highest Destiny Path.

A Guide to Freedom, Enlightenment and Peace, the writings in this book inspire us upon an Illumined Pathway to realize our Full Potential. They unveil the Secret Code to our True Destiny. These Sacred Writings reveal the Majesty and Power of our Innate Divinity and speak to the extraordinary mission we have come to Earth to fulfill at this significant time. Eloquently written through Letters from the Inner Self, this book is destined to help awaken and inspire humanity in its next evolutionary leap in consciousness, igniting Positive World Change and a planetary transformation unparalleled in history, restoring Eden on Earth.

# TheQuest
## Heal Your Life, Change Your Destiny

## A Breakthrough Self Healing System

"This book will ignite a Revolution In Consciousness
so powerful, it could restore Peace on Earth."

"People would not choose to stay in pain
if they knew this was available."

In this groundbreaking book, Dr. Ariel unveils her breakthrough Healing System, the 7 Master Keys to Inner Peace, and a powerful Life Mastery Path. She demystifies the psyche like no other work has done and provides tools to quickly resolve issues, restore harmony in relationships, master your psychology, and heal the scars from your painful past.

Through years of pioneering work in the 'uncharted realms' of the psyche, she made many landmark discoveries, uncovered the cause of suffering, and developed a cure that could change the destiny of the planet.

Distilled into seven powerful steps, TheQuest is designed to accelerate a personal and planetary transformation that could help end suffering on Earth. Inspiring a Journey of Self Discovery that is empowering and life changing, TheQuest unlocks the Secret Code to your True Identity and provides a Key to Actualizing your Full Potential.

Sign up to get the E-book FREE
at http://www.AuroraJulianaAriel.com

# Aurora's Solo Music CD

## Renaissance of Grace

*The exotic vocals of Aurora with Bruce BecVar
weave a mystical blend that is both uplifting and inspiring,
transporting us into a world of transcendence and light.*

Talented musicians grace this gypsy world music album including renowned multi-instrumentalist, Bruce BecVar; Percussionist Rafael Padilla; Peruvian Shaman, Tito La Rosa on Andean Pan Pipes; Gypsy Violinist, Don Lax; Violinist Rachel Handlin, Michael Buono on drums, and Brian BecVar on Synthesizer. Purchase through AEOS at http://www.AEOS.ws

*"Aurora Juliana Ariel is one of those rare artists whose clear voice and beautiful music transmit to more than just the ear, but reaches into the listener's heart with hidden healing messages. Coupled with the extraordinary talent of musician/composer Bruce BecVar, Aurora's offering awakens our inner peace and invites our own calm center to bubble up to the surface. Aurora's mystical language is at once both exotic and familiar, adventurous and comforting. Renaissance of Grace, as one of the song titles indicates, is truly a Journey Of The Heart: one pleasurable piece of music after another that you will never want to end. The work as a whole lives up to its name."*
-Pamela Polland, **Award Winning Recording Artist, Vocal Coach**

*"Journey of the Heart and Shiva Moon are two of the most heartfelt ballads you will hear on any release, their voices soaring together and weaving in and out of fluid guitar lines, gentle piano, bass flute, and percussion. The lyrical romanticism that is expressed owes much to the spirit of Aurora Juliana Ariel, who collaborates with Bruce BecVar to create inspired songs."* —DL, New Age Voice

# Gypsy Soul, Heart of Passion

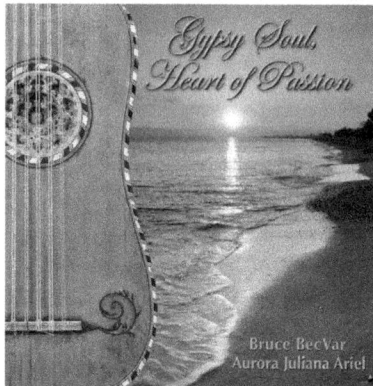

## Bruce BecVar & Aurora

*Fast paced Nuevo Flamenco Songs
drop into slower, exotic melodies...
As Bruce BecVar's master guitarmanship
weaves a mystical blend of vocals and
gypsy guitar with the transcendent vocals of Aurora
amid violin, pan flutes, and percussion by
a host of illustrious musicians*

Talented musicians grace this gypsy world music album including renowned multi-instrumentalist, Bruce BecVar; Percussionist Rafael Padilla; Peruvian Shaman, Tito La Rosa on Andean Pan Pipes; Gypsy Violinist – Don Lax; Rachel Handlin and Charlie Bisharat on violins, Michael Buono on piano, Steve Reid on percussion, Brandon Fields and Richard Hardy on Saxophone, and Brian BecVar on Synthesizer.

*"This album is a therapeutic blend of New Age musical sound graced by the angelic voice of Ariel who is not without her match in BecVar. Ariel and Becvar put together a musical experience worth cherishing. The album's music is relaxingly invigorating and will stimulate you with its deep thought and meaning. An inspiring, earnest and spiritual journey is what you're about to embark on. Think Strunz and Farah on a spiritual path."* --**Manny Auguste, Bryan Farrish Radio Promotion.**

# River of Gold

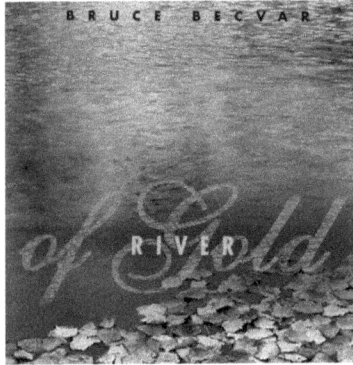

## Bruce BecVar & Aurora

*This music uplifts and inspires, enchants and awakens,
and keeps you coming back for more!*

A brilliant collaboration, River of Gold is a magical weave of guitar, instrumentals, and exotic vocals, this album has been highly acclaimed for the SPECTACULAR LOVE and TRANSCENDENT JOY that fills every note, carrying you into a world of romance, beauty and light.

*"Journey of the Heart and Shiva Moon are two of the most heartfelt ballads you will hear on any release, their voices soaring together and weaving in and out of fluid guitar lines, gentle piano, bass, flute, and percussion. The lyrical romanticism that is expressed owes much to the spirit of Aurora Juliana Ariel, who collaborates with Bruce BecVar to create inspired songs."* ~ **DL, New Age Voice**

*"The sweet duet "Journey of the Heart" is a dance of masculine and feminine voices delicately interspersed with exquisite guitar rhythms. As I listen to this and other pieces, I am transported to a land where love and romance abound and the beauty of nature flows through my heart like a river of gold. This recording is deeply passionate, exotic, and simply unforgettable."* ~ **Betty Timm**

*"BecVar generates electricity in partnership with vocalist and coproducer Aurora. Abundantly intimate, this album is nothing less than a magnificent mash note, a Valentine that all can share."* **–PJ Birosik**

www.ingramcontent.com/pod-product-compliance
Lightning Source LLC
Chambersburg PA
CBHW060018100426

42740CB00010B/1514